Dane Love is the author of numerous books on Scottish local history. He was born in Cumnock but now lives in the countryside near Auchinleck. He is descended from Robin Love, who fought for Bonnie Prince Charlie at the battles of Prestonpans and Culloden. A member of Ayrshire Archaeological and Nat... ...ety, he is also the Honorary Secretary of the Scottish Covenanter Memorials Associat... ...ntiquaries of Scotland. He works as a Principal Teacher at Irvine Royal Acaden... ...travelling around Scotland, visiting histo...

Hugh Baird's blacksmith and farrier premises, 8-12 Back Street, c. 1900.

Title Page and Back Cover: Ordnance Survey Six Inch Map of Kilmarnock in 1896.
Following Page: Ayrshire Clearance Stores shop, 22 Waterloo Street, around 1936.

A Look Back at
KILMARNOCK

Dane Love

CARN PUBLISHING

© Dane Love, 2022.
First Published in Great Britain, 2022.

ISBN - 978 1 911043 16 4

Published by Carn Publishing Ltd.,
Lochnoran House,
Auchinleck,
Ayrshire, KA18 3JW.

www.carnpublishing.com

Printed by Bell & Bain Ltd.,
Glasgow, G46 7UQ.

The right of the author to be identified as the author of this work has been asserted by him in accordance with the Copyright, Designs and Patents Act, 1988.

All rights reserved. No part of this publication can be reproduced, stored, or transmitted in any form, or by any means, electronic, mechanical or photocopying, recording or otherwise, without the express written permission of the publisher.

Introduction

Kilmarnock is one of the three largest towns in Ayrshire, indeed, for a time it was the largest by population, and its industry made it famous across the world, especially concerning whisky, but also in its manufacture of locomotives, water control castings and carpets. Today, the town has a population of around 47,000, and though the major industries of the past have more or less gone, it is still the administrative centre of East Ayrshire, commercial hub of the district and shopping destination.

When Kilmarnock was founded can no longer be determined – it perhaps owes its name to St Marnock, who may have established a cell here, but the earliest reference to a community is perhaps from the twelfth century, when the Lockharts built a church, long under the curacy of Kilwinning Abbey. The town started to grow with the formation of the church, and in 1591 it was created a burgh of barony for Lord Boyd, allowing a market. Competition with Irvine was always serious, for Irvine was a Royal Burgh and was protective of its port and market privileges for Cunninghame, in which jurisdiction Kilmarnock was located. In the seventeenth century the town had a weekly market, manufactured bonnets and 'Scottish cloth', but the houses were described in 1658 as 'little better than huts'. These were all destroyed in May 1668 when a large fire raged through the community.

A few years after the Glorious Revolution, in 1700, Kilmarnock residents bought the rights to the burgh, and the town advanced consistently from that point. Carpet making was introduced in 1777, rising to twelve manufacturers at one time. Kilmarnock Bank was founded in 1802, subsequently merging with Hunters of Ayr and in 1843 becoming part of the Union Bank of Scotland. The Glasgow and South Western Railway Company moved its engineering works to Bonnyton in 1856.

In the early nineteenth century the burgh was greatly developed, and the town improvement committee realised that the old and narrow streets were hindering potential trade and development. Accordingly, a plan for new grid-based streets was made, resulting in the great thoroughfares of King Street, Titchfield Street, John Finnie Street and surrounding roadways. The full course of this development was never completed, leaving many of the older streets and lanes within the grid, such as Bank Street, Croft Street and Nelson Street, out of kilter with the plan.

The new streets were developed with lines of commercial properties, and today John Finnie Street remains one of the most complete examples of Victorian architecture in Scotland, whereas King Street was considerably redeveloped in 1975, when pedestrianisation and inside shopping became the fashion. This resulted in new blocks of commercial premises being built where once the town hall and other buildings stood, and the large indoor Burns Precinct replaced the architectural splendour of Duke Street.

The major industries of the town include the railway works off West Langlands Street and Bonnyton Road, Andrew Barclay, Sons & Co. Ltd. producing locomotives that were sold across the world from 1840. Glenfield and Kennedy still produce water valves and other water control equipment, whereas Johnnie Walker's whisky blending and bottling plant and bonded warehouses have been closed, international owners relocating the business away from the town where John Walker blended and sold his first whisky in 1820. Blackwood's produced woollen garments and yarns for years, and in 1908 Robert Blackwood formed a partnership with Gavin Morton, establishing Blackwood and Morton of Kilmarnock, better known as BMK, manufacturing carpets. The business closed in 2005. Shoes were made by Saxone and Clark's. At Moorfield a giant tractor factory was built by Massey Harris in 1949, later Massey Ferguson, but it was closed in 1980.

Coal was mined in the vicinity of the town, former mines being located within the extent of the present community, at Grange, Bonnyton and Portland. Quarrying took place at Dean, Holm and elsewhere, and clay was worked into bricks and tiles at Gargieston. Clay was also made into sanitary ware at Hillhead, Longpark, and Bonnyton, the products being exported extensively. Although reliant on heavy industry, the town also had a number of nurseries, at Westmoor, Holmes, Burnside, New Park and New Pit, among others, producing garden produce.

Leisure for Kilmarnock folk often involves sport, and Kilmarnock Football Club was formed in 1869 and continues to enjoy success at their home ground of Rugby Park. It is now the oldest professional football club in Scotland. The club won the Scottish league in 1965, the Scottish League Cup in 2012, and the Scottish Cup in 1920, 1929 and 1997. Various parks in the town allow quieter recreation, including the Howard Park (gifted to the town by Lady Howard de Walden in 1893) and Kay Park (opened 1879). Golf can be played at Annanhill, opened on 27 April 1954, or Kilmarnock Municipal Golf Course at Caprington (opened 1909). Kilmarnock Cricket Club was formed in 1852. Bowling clubs exist at London Road (Kilmarnock Bowling Club, formed 1740), Portland (1860), Townholm (1870), North West Kilmarnock, Bellfield and Riccarton.

Kilmarnock has lived through Scotland's history, including the Covenanting period of the seventeenth century, Tam Dalyell making Dean Castle his headquarters, and John Nisbet was executed at The Cross in April 1683 for his Covenanting adherences. In the Laigh Kirkyard is a memorial to Nisbet, and a second to John Ross and John Shields, executed in Edinburgh in 1666, and also to the Kilmarnock Covenanters who drowned in a shipwreck at Orkney in 1679. The Jacobite period is remembered for the association of William Boyd, 4th Earl of Kilmarnock, a strong supporter of Bonnie Prince Charlie, who was executed on 18 August 1746. Ten years before this, Dean Castle had been destroyed by fire, leaving it a ruin until it was restored by the 8th Lord Howard de Walden. The first printing of Robert Burns' Poems, Chiefly in the Scottish Dialect, was carried out in Kilmarnock, making the town an important place in Burns' history.

JAMES LETHAM
TEMPLE
A. F. McQUAT
MANUFACTURING CHEMISTS.
ESTABLISHED 1798
CHEMISTS
A77
A71
A77
A735

The Cross Looking West

This postcard view of Kilmarnock Cross dates from the 1950s and was taken from the upstairs window of the Portland Arms Hotel, looking south-westwards down Cheapside Street towards the Laigh Kirk tower. Kilmarnock Cross is the recognised centre of the town, and here the original market place was located, and the old gallows, although it was probably only used when the Covenanters were executed. The town grew up around the cross, and roads departed from it in six directions, making it an exceptionally busy junction. Different methods of controlling traffic flow have been used over the years, and at the time of this image a roundabout was used. In 1975 the cross was closed to traffic and the area pedestrianised. On the left of the picture is the baronial building located between Duke and Waterloo streets. The ground floor is occupied by the Temple Bar, latterly The Hub, with A. F. McQuat's Castle Restaurant next door. On the ground in front of McQuat's a setting of stones marked the site of the gallows, where the Covenanting martyr, John Nisbet in Glen farm, near Darvel, was executed on either 4 or 14 April 1683 – there is confusion as to which date is correct. On the other side of the narrow Waterloo Street is the corner of Lewis's shop. This was owned by Lewis Isaac and had no connection with Lewis's in Glasgow. On King Street is Claude Alexander's tailor's shop. John Cameron & Son were jewellers and watch-makers, having been at this spot since at least 1860. They were noted for the manufacture of many local sporting trophies, including the Ayrshire Football Association silver vase of 1877. Rankin & Borland were old-established druggists and manufacturing chemists, established in 1798. The firm made treatments for animals and also made and sold aerated waters. The factory was located in East George Street, and in addition to 'Vita Crush' mineral waters, they were also licensed to bottle Gaymer's cider. The building at the corner they occupied was previously the Rainbow Hotel. Cheapside Street leads down to Bank Street, with the Laigh Kirk steeple being dominant. At the corner of Cheapside with Portland Street was the premises of David Lauder's Ironmongers. This too was an old-established business, founded in 1901.

A Look Back at KILMARNOCK ~ page 9

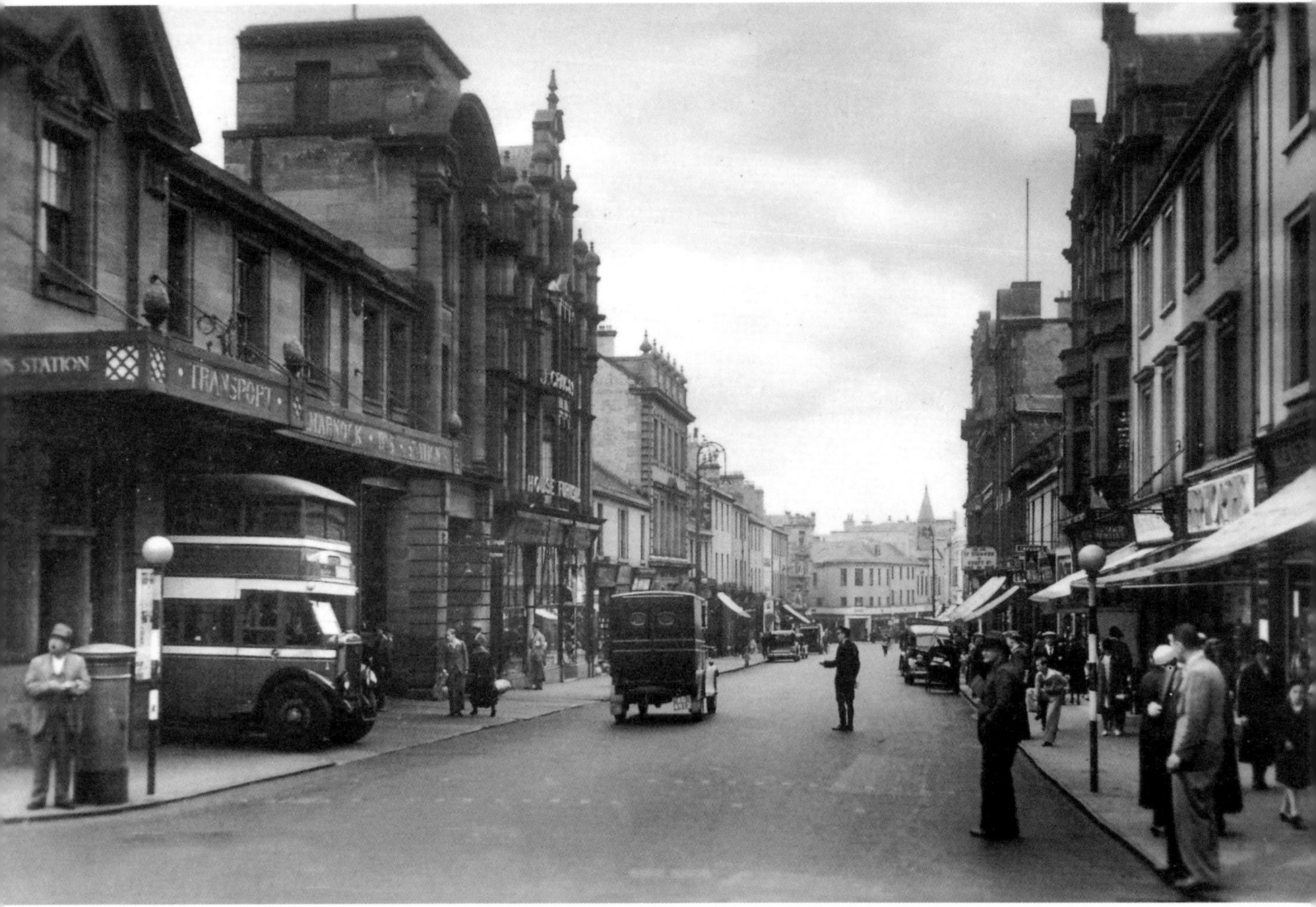
STATION
TRANSPORT

Portland Street

Portland Street dates from around 1816, having been cut through some older premises on the north side of The Cross to form a new main road into the town from Glasgow and places to the north. It was named in honour of the local landowner, the 4th Duke of Portland (1768-1854). Developments took a number of years to come to fruition, for example, in 1823 'that new inn in Portland Street of Kilmarnock, belonging to the Merchants' Society, consisting of five rooms on the first floor, four on the second, and thirteen bedrooms on the third' was offered to let. This was the George Hotel. This postcard view is of the southern half of the street, looking from George Street towards The Cross. On the left is Western Scottish's omnibus depot. This was opened in 1923 and as can be seen, had a garage capable of taking double-decker buses. The bus station remained in use until 1974, when the present bus station at the top of the Foregate was opened. The bus station building was demolished in 1979. Following it was John Craig & Son's furniture warehouse. This was one of Kilmarnock's finest buildings, constructed of red sandstone and highly ornamented on its upper floors. It was designed by Andrew & Newlands. An older building follows, and then the four-floor banking premises of the Bank of Scotland. This was closed in 1986. More traditional nineteenth century buildings follow, their ground floors occupied by shops, the upper floors by either offices or flats. Lewis's building is seen at The Cross, and then we see the west side of the street. The tall building with the bay windows was originally a branch of the Kilmarnock Equitable Co-operative Society Ltd. This was built of Ballochmyle sandstone and was opened in November 1905. It was designed by Gabriel Andrew and contained a grocery on the ground floor and furniture store above. The facade was meant to be retained in the new developments in Portland Street, but it was demolished in 1990 and only the two carved figures, representing 'Industry' and 'Justice', were saved, now located in a pillar in the car park at the top of the street. Part of the street's redevelopment was named Portland Gate.

HEPWORTHS
66
RSMcColl
D. M. HANNAH & SONS
H. G. McKELVIE & SON
HG Mc KELVIE & SON

Portland Street Shops

This photograph shows two buildings in Portland Street prior to their demolition in 1989. The left-hand block contained The Hosiery Shop, one of two branches in Kilmarnock (the other being at 46 King Street). This company was based in Irvine and grew to have over sixty shops across the country. One of the earliest occupants of the premises, up to 1845, was Thomas Miller, baker and confectioner. It was then occupied by Thomas Lang, seedsman, then Mrs Cunningham, confectioner and pastry baker. In 1899 William Paterson opened the Portland Restaurant there, with 'commodious and comfortable rooms, especially the large room suitable for meetings' and the 'comfortable dining room one stair up'. Next door is the newsagent shop of R. S. McColl. In the 1850s, this was occupied by Robert Sturrock, who was a grocer and wine merchant. In 1862 ownership changed to George Morison & Sons, who also had a steam fruit preserve works. The firm would send you a 'sample tin, 14lb strawberry jam' on receipt of six shillings and sixpence of postage stamps. By the 1880s the shop was Hugh Gemmill's ironmongery warehouse, and in 1920 it was converted into Hepworth's gentlemen's outfitters. This business sold men's clothing and had rooms on the first floor – the name of the shop can still be seen on the façade. D. M. Hannah & Sons moved into the shop shown in 1926 and remained there until the building was scheduled for demolition, after which they opened up in College Wynd in 1989. A traditional grocery, the shop also sold wine and spirits and their delivery van is parked in the street. Unfortunately, in 2008 the company closed down. Prior to Hannah's, in the 1830s until 1848, this was Andrew Papple's grocery and spirits shop, followed by Alexander Erskine. H. G. McKelvie & Son was a butcher, established in this shop in the 1930s. The business remained until around 1989. Prior to McKelvie's the shop was run by James Cunningham, and before that (in the 1870s) it was Thomas Paton's flesher shop. In 1860 William Dick had established his butcher's or flesher's business there, one that he claimed had been on the go for a century and a half.

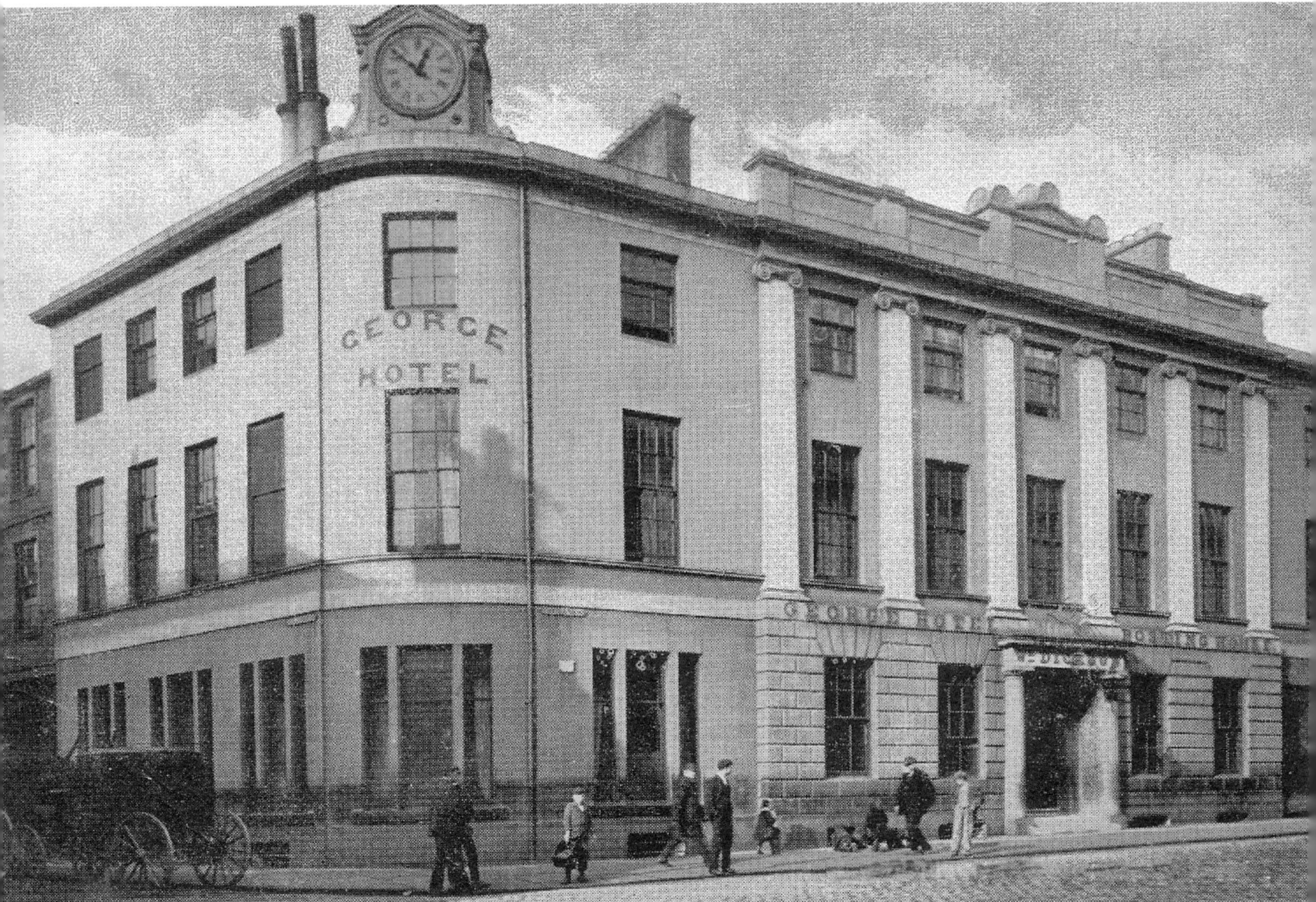
GEORGE
HOTEL

George Hotel

The George Hotel was erected at the corner of George Street and Portland Street in 1823. It has been speculated that the Glasgow architect, John Thomson, designed the building, distinguished by its six Ionic pilasters and a public clock over the curving façade. Originally a coaching inn with posting facilities, the hotel was to serve as the town's premier place for accommodation for many years. In June 1849 the hotel was sold by the Merchants' Company of Kilmarnock, at which time there were four parlours on the ground floor, four on the first floor and twelve bedrooms on the third floor. In 1860 the hotel's posting establishment had 12 horses, 2 hearses, 4 Harringtons, 1 coach, 2 omnibuses, 6 dog-carts, 2 gigs and 1 cab. The hotel had a large function room, which was superior to the town hall, and as a result it was used for civic receptions. Amongst those who stayed in the hotel were Ensign Charles Ewart, a locally-born hero of Waterloo; philanthropist, Andrew Carnegie; and Andrew Fisher, Crosshouse-born Prime Minister of Australia. Here also the local masonic lodges, St John's Masonic Lodge (established in 1735) and St Andrew's Masonic Lodge (established in 1771), met. Various church denominations used the hotel's hall prior to acquiring their own premises. These included the Morisonian Congregational Church (1841), Roman Catholic Church (1846), and Grange Free Church (1876). The hotel was home to Kilmarnock Burns Club from 1841 and the Burns Federation was founded here at a meeting held on 17 July 1885, the hotel's landlord, George Aird, being a keen Burnsian. William Wallace & Co. owned the inn for a time – they were whisky blenders in the town, being bought by Johnnie Walker in 1912. The hotel closed in 1920 and was converted into commercial premises. The former hall and part of the building was reconstructed as the George Cinema, opening in 1923. The building was erected on the site of the former inn belonging to Sandy Patrick, son-in-law of Tam Samson, and thus it was frequented on occasion by Robert Burns. Adjoining this was a bowling green, where Kilmarnock Bowling Club was established in 1740. Today the former hotel is mainly occupied by Mason Murphy furniture retailers, a business that has been in existence since 1873.

A Look Back at KILMARNOCK ~ *page 15*

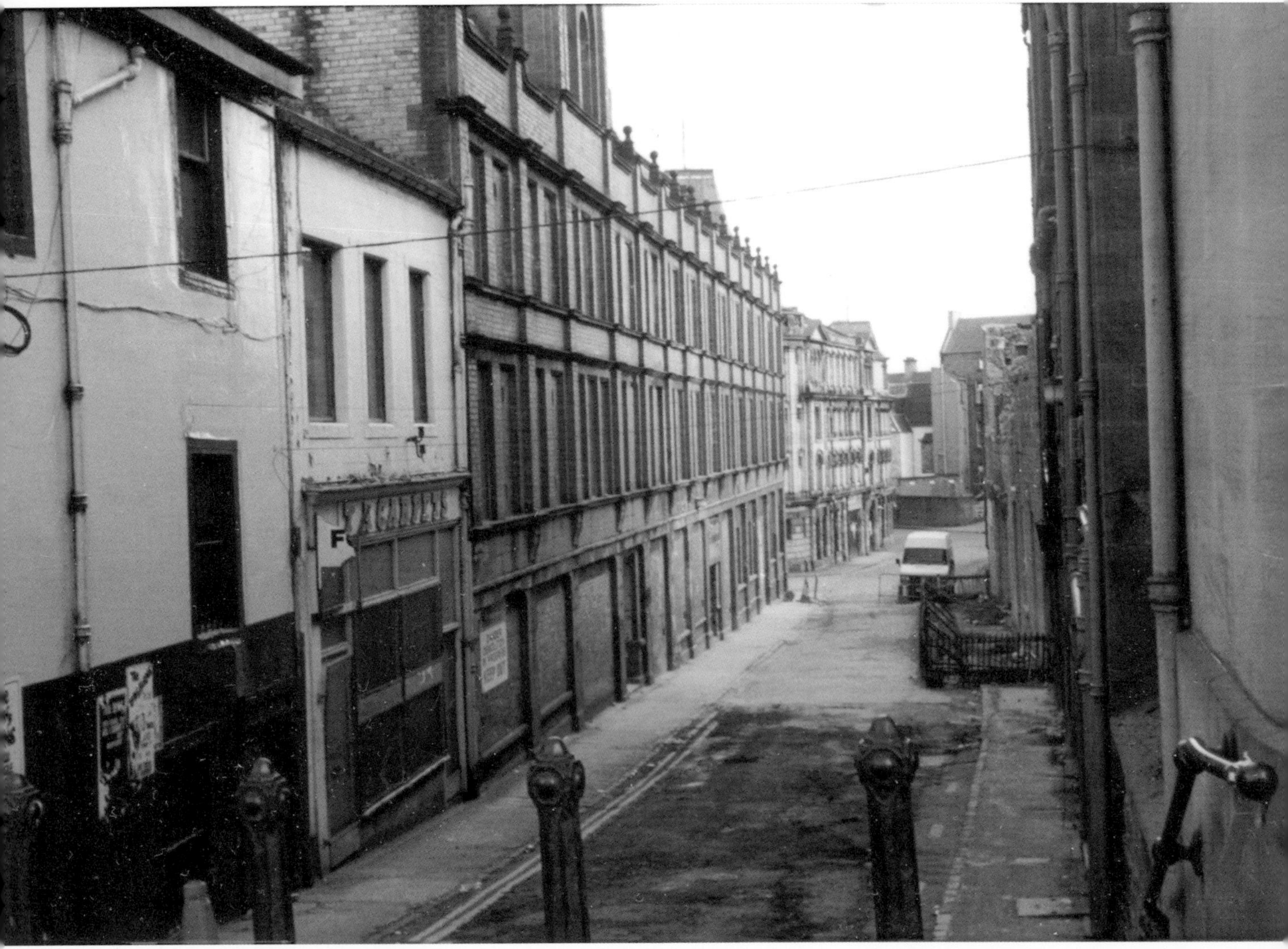

Strand Street

Strand Street is an old roadway in the centre of town, leading from Cheapside Street near the Cross to the steps at West George Street. According to Mackay's *History of Kilmarnock*, this was 'one of the earliest streets of the town. Though latterly occupied by the poorer classes, it was the residence of some of the wealthier families during the last [eighteenth] century.' It is reckoned that Strand Street was the first street in the town to be paved using rounded stones taken from the river, this being 1708. This image was taken from the steps looking down along the length of the Johnnie Walker whisky bonds. The first building on the left is part of the Glasgow and South West Railway Tavern, now Fanny by Gaslight. The small shop, number 51, was at the time of the photograph occupied by T. A. Carpets. In the mid-1850s it was occupied by a smithy and by 1872 it was owned by Robert Paton, smith and ironmonger. The red-brick whisky bonds follow. On the right-hand side of the street are the rear facades of the former Ossington Hotel. Before John Finnie Street was laid out, this was the site of Langlands House. In the second half of the eighteenth century, it was the property of William Park, surgeon, then James Dunlop, who owned some land around it. Gradually it was surrounded by buildings, including Dunlop Street, which was named after the proprietor. Later owners included James Rankin, chief magistrate of Kilmarnock, Joseph Thomson, baker and grain dealer, and Frederick Kershaw, probably the last occupant before it was demolished. Other buildings that existed in the street include the Unionist Rooms, erected in 1891. At the bottom end, where the A1 bus garage was opened in the 1950s, stood the Crown Inn and Hotel. In the nineteenth century this was an important posting establishment and it had a large hall, bakehouse with two ovens, coachhouse, stables, and offices. Inside were an 'American Ten Pin Alley' and a rifle shooting gallery. Opposite the Crown Inn was a line of buildings forming the west side of the street, with the Kirk Lane behind. These were demolished in 1876 to widen the roadway when John Dickie Street was created.

A Look Back at KILMARNOCK ~ page 17

WHEATSHEAF
HOTEL
DANGER
DEMOLITION
IN PROGRESS
KEEP OUT
LOUNGE

Croft Street

Croft Street is one of the older streets of Kilmarnock, predating Portland Street by over a century. It was probably one of the original routes from Kilmarnock Cross towards Stewarton. It may have existed in the seventeenth century. This view was taken in the 1980s and is looking north-west towards Strand Street. On the right is the Wheatsheaf Inn, one of the town's longest-lasting hostelries. Being set-back from the street would indicate that it perhaps predates the creation of the route, and that it was at one time a free-standing building. On the two gables can be seen the old Scots form of building, where crow steps, or corbie-steps have been used. There were a number of old buildings around Kilmarnock town centre built in this way. The Wheatsheaf Inn was a posting establishment, and to the right-hand side of it was a gate that led to a large yard which had stables. Landlords over the years included Mrs Robb in the 1850s and A. P. Kerr in the 1950s. In 1988-90 the inn was redeveloped, and much of the old part was removed. The façade was retained, though internally the pub occupies one of the new shop units facing Portland Street, where the main entrance is now located. There were a few other inns in Croft Street, on the opposite side of the road being the Commercial Inn. This was a common stop off point for carriers and farmers attending market. At the Portland Street end was the Black Bull Inn and at the Strand Street corner was another public house. Yet another stood behind where the wooden fence is in the picture. The gable with the arched bricks in the centre of the image was a bonded warehouse used by Johnnie Walker. It was demolished in 1992. The firm's first bonded warehouse was opened in this street in 1873. The building on the left side of the street survives as offices for East Ayrshire Council, converted for such purposes in 2009-11. It was erected in 1897 to plans by Gabriel Andrew for Johnnie Walker. The buildings, which held extensive quantities of spirits, were built to be as fireproof as possible.

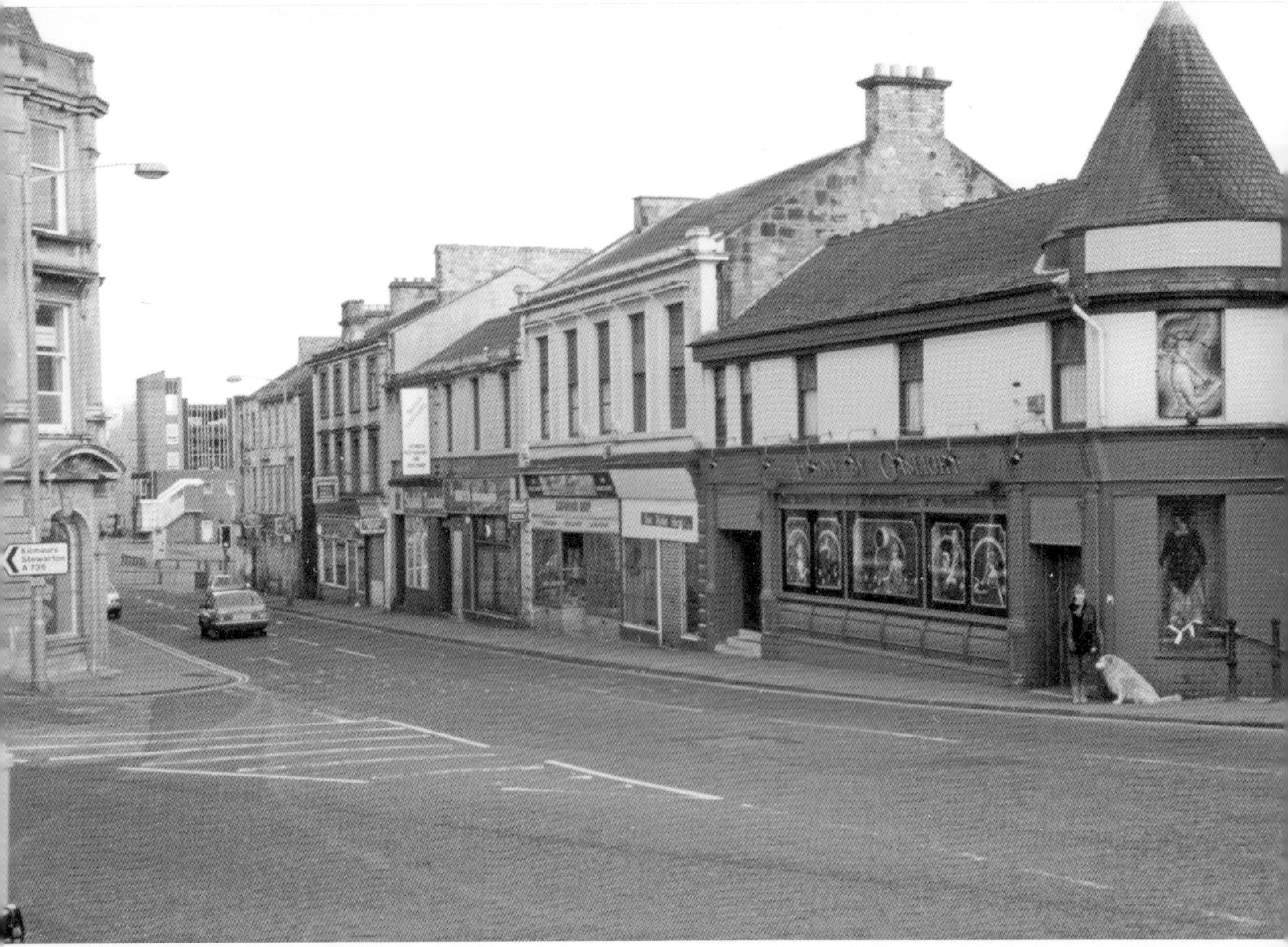
Kilmaurs
Stewarton
A 735

West George Street

Although one of Kilmarnock's shorter streets, West George Street is one of the busiest, being part of the inner ring road. The street was originally laid out in 1830. This image was taken from the end of Garden Street, at the foot of the railway station embankment, looking east towards the junction of Portland Street. The building on the immediate right was the Glasgow and South Western Railway Tavern, established in 1846 and now known as Fanny by Gaslight, still a public house. Next door, the pair of shops was erected in the mid nineteenth century. One of the shops, owned by Sinforiani Brothers (Mario, Alessandro and Davide), has been retailing from the same premises since 1931. Previously it was William Bechelli's café, and there was a billiard hall upstairs. The Sinforiani's ran the café until 1981, after which it continued as a newsagent and they expanded the whisky and alcohol sales. The buildings beyond were demolished in 1994 and were replaced by a lower, double-storey Gala bingo hall, opened in 1999. The two-storey building with the large sign was for many years Alexanders' Stores, at the time of the picture Mecca bookmakers and Shabab tandoori. Next door was the three-storey block that contained the George Bar and Henderson's Restaurant, originally a temperance establishment. After a narrow lane was the Bob Inn (originally the Waverley Inn), before Portland Street struck off to the right. East George Street continued on, now totally removed and the parking area at the top of Portland Street occupies the site. On the north side of West George Street, seen to the left of this picture, the ornamental building belonged to the Prudential Assurance Company, erected in a narrow gusset site between West George Street and Garden Street. It was later an estate agency and is currently the WG13 restaurant. In the upper floors were the drawing offices of James Hay and Steel, architects. Further down the street on the same side were the George Hotel's Assembly Rooms, latterly the Billiard Rooms, the building subsequently demolished and the George Picture House, erected in 1922 to plans by Hay & Steel, built over it and on the site of the hotel's stabling. This became the Hippodrome nightclub and has had a few other names since.

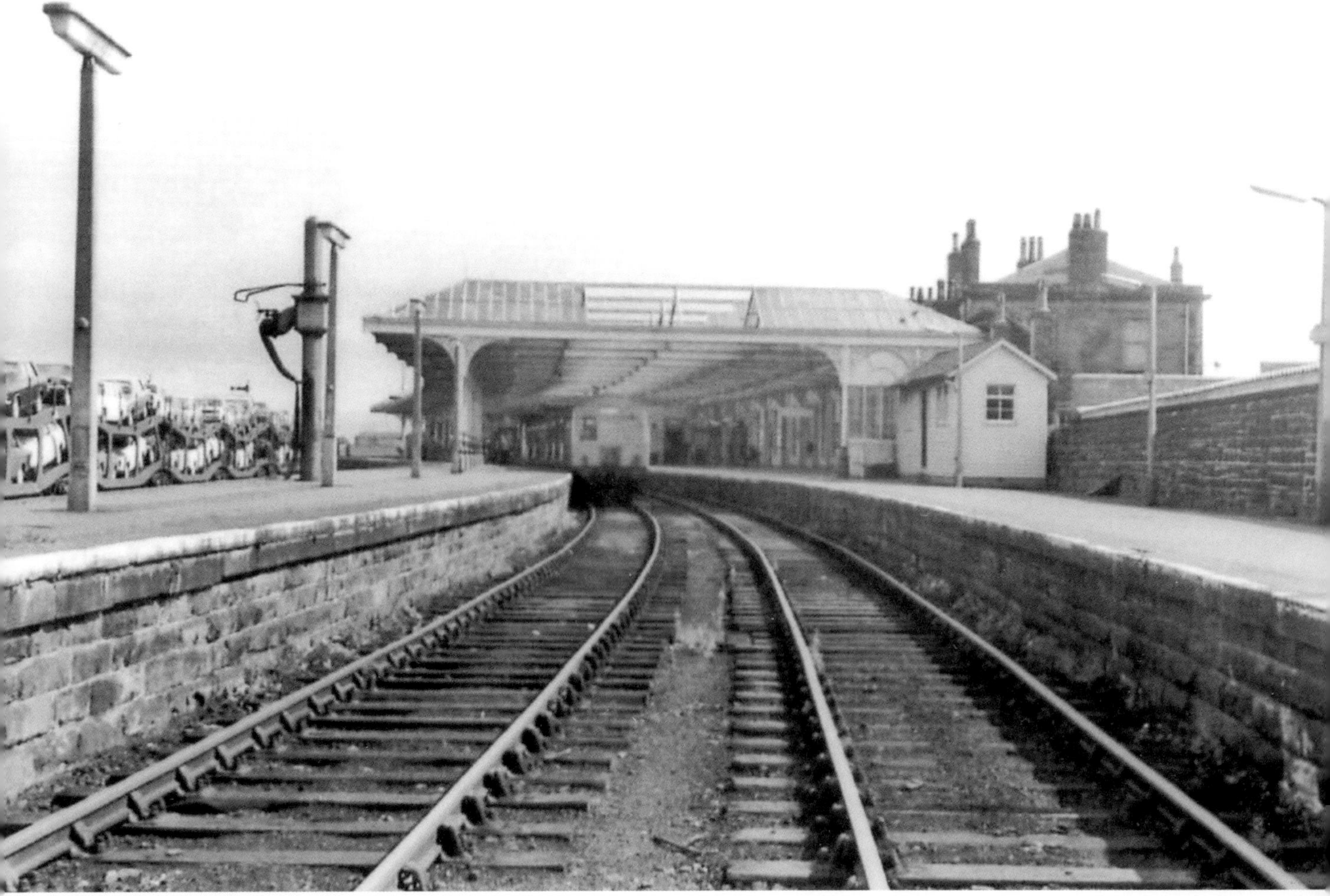

Railway Station

Located on elevated ground at the top of John Finnie Street is Kilmarnock Railway Station. The Glasgow, Paisley, Kilmarnock & Ayr Railway Company developed a line south from Glasgow, reaching the town in 1843. The station was originally opened on 4 April, and was located slightly further west of the present buildings. The line was continued southwards, crossing the top of the town by a 23-arched viaduct over the valley of the Kilmarnock Water, and when it linked with the line from Dumfries on 28 October 1850 the railway company became the Glasgow and South-Western Railway Company, which it remained until 1923. The present station platforms and buildings were erected in 1873-77, after the Glasgow and South Western Railway created a new line through Stewarton. The architect was probably Andrew Galloway, and the Italianate tower is a prominent landmark in the townscape. During construction work, Patrick Bradley was killed when a wagon ran over him. The goods yards and sheds were located to the north and south of the passenger station, extensive sidings and yards covering a large area. At one time there was a second station in Kilmarnock, though technically it was in Riccarton. The Riccarton & Craigie Station was established on the Gatehead and Hurlford branch line, which was opened on 14 July 1904. The station was positioned to the west of Campbell Street, and the Goods Station was to the east of Academy Street. This station was never regularly used. In 1935 the town council tried to get the railway company to open the station at weekends, to assist in transporting the hundreds of residents who wished to go to the beaches of Ayr and Prestwick, but this came to nought. There was actually an older railway line in Kilmarnock – the line that extended from Kilmarnock House to Troon. This was authorised on 27 May 1808 and was opened on 6 July 1812. It was built by the Duke of Portland to transport coal from the district to the harbour. Passenger services were introduced to it in 1812. Much of the line survives, but the original terminus and last few hundred yards have gone. Only a couple of angled fencelines between properties at Ellis and Seaford streets indicate the route of the line.

A Look Back at KILMARNOCK ~ *page 23*

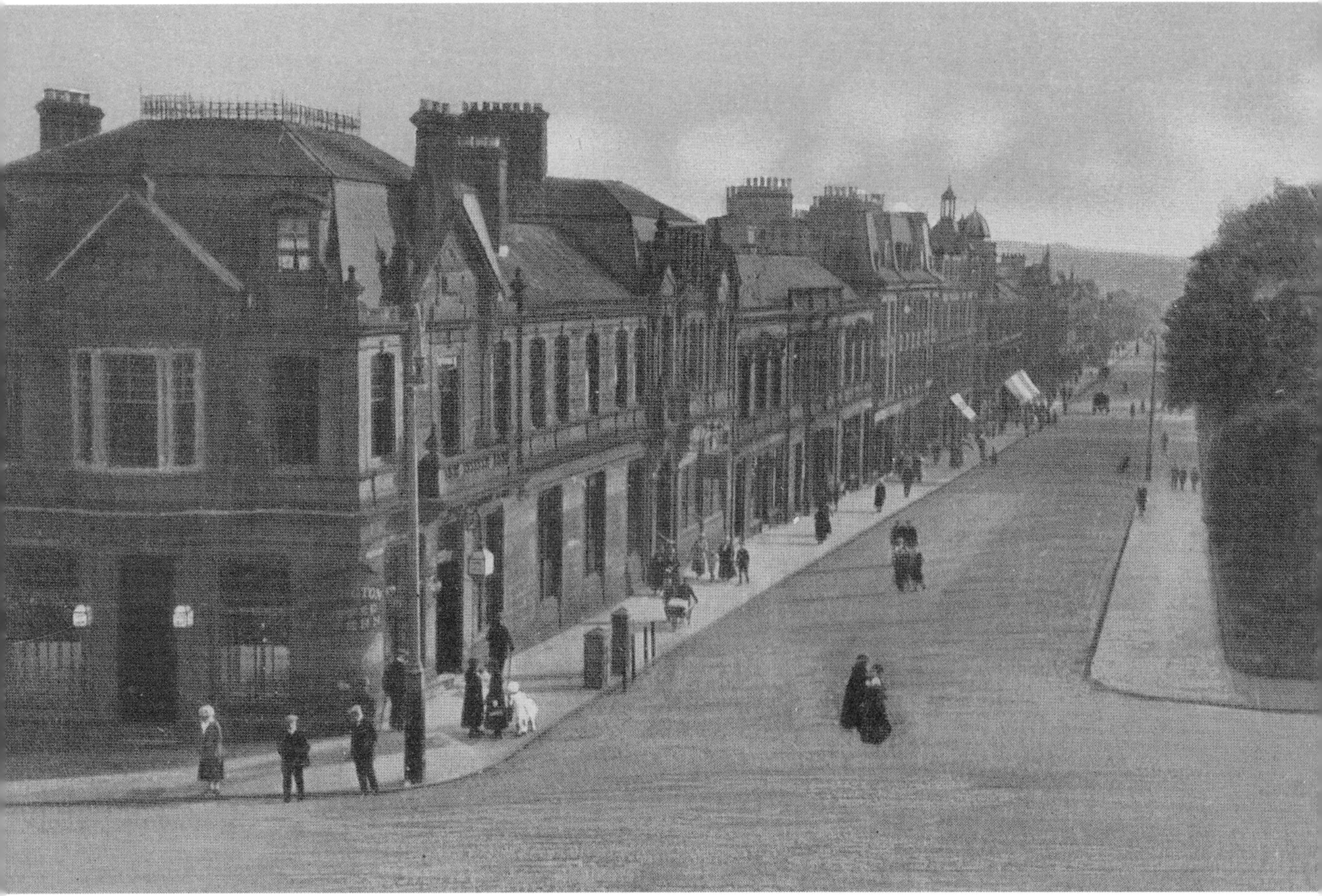

John Finnie Street

John Finnie Street was one of Kilmarnock's finest developments. Previously, this part of town was occupied by a random tapestry of houses and gardens, with narrow and irregular streets criss-crossing the area. A straight line was drawn from the railway station south towards the Court House, a distance of around one quarter of a mile, and through time the properties were bought up and the 64 feet wide roadway laid out by the Town Improvement Trustees. There was some difficulty in establishing the route, but John Finnie of Bowdon Lodge, Manchester, stepped in and underwrote the proceedings. The street was opened on 26 October 1864, when a half holiday was declared in the burgh. Following a parade of bands along the street, a banquet was held in the town hall. This picture shows the street as viewed from the north end, from West George Street south towards Dunlop Street (one of the old streets that predated John Finnie Street). The building at the end was number 26 West George Street. At number 4 was the Ossington Hotel, erected to plans by John & Robert Samson Ingram in 1883-84. This was originally a temperance hotel. It was owned by Lady Charlotte Ossington, daughter of the Duke of Portland. She was married to John Evelyn Denison (1800-1873) who was created Viscount Ossington in 1872. Denison had served as a member of parliament for fifty years and was Speaker in the House of Commons from 1857-72. The hotel was bought by Kilmarnock Town Council in 1967 for £18,000. It was then let to the existing manager, John Ross, who renamed it the Ross Hotel. In later years it changed hands regularly, no longer being a hotel but bar and disco. Names included La Toc, O'Donnell's, Ossington's (1978-1982) and The Tartan Sheep (2018). Next door, at number 6-12, was the Operetta House. Designed in the Italianate style, it had seating for 1,500 spectators. The building cost £7,000 to erect. The Operetta House was never to be too successful, being unprofitable. It closed in 1925. It was later converted into St John's United Free Church. It became an auction house and then a public house. Robert Ingram also designed the premises at 14-28 (dating from 1880), and the three-storey block at 30-38 (1895-96).

A Look Back at KILMARNOCK ~ *page 25*

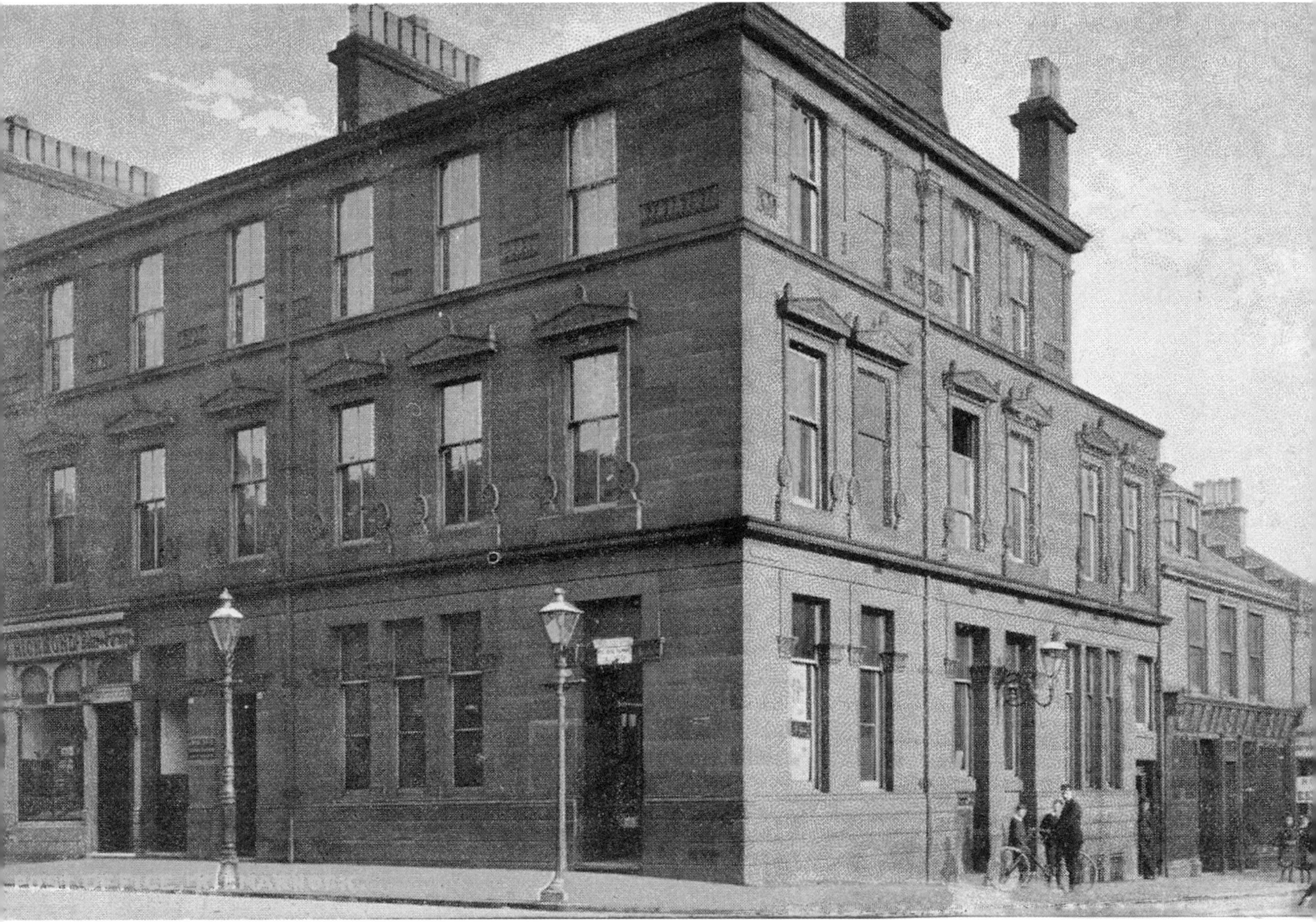

Old Post Office

Located at the corner of John Finnie Street and Bank Place, this building was for a time the post office. It was opened in May 1877 and gradually extended into the first floor, but was latterly very much cramped. At that time the postal service in Kilmarnock delivered 42,285 letters per week. It was built to plans by the Kilmarnock architect, William Railton, for Bailie Muir. In style, the building was influenced by Alexander 'Greek' Thomson. Within the buildings was also the town chamberlain's office, as well as the police constabulary office. The first post office in Kilmarnock was located at the Cross. The first mail-coach to pass through Kilmarnock did not arrive until 1787. This service only commenced following a letter of appeal from the council to the Postmaster General, resulting in a service from Carlisle to Glasgow passing through. The first mail-coach was the 'Camperdown'. The office relocated to Market Lane and then to a building in Queen Street. A new office in Queen Street was opened on Friday 25 November 1859, located in a building erected by John Bicket. Never large enough, a new office was opened at 92 King Street, but it was closed when the post office in the picture was opened. A new post office building was erected on the west side of John Finnie Street in 1907, at the corner of Nelson Street, and opened for business on 26 November. The building took nine months to erect. The building was designed by W. T. Oldrieve, principal architect to the Post Office. The first letter posted there was sent by the postmaster, J. MacIntyre, to Provost Gemmill. In 1907 the average number of letters delivered in Kilmarnock was 112,000. In 1907 the post office had 81 employees in Kilmarnock. The post office remained in this building until it was closed around 2015. Today, post office services are carried out by an agency in W. H. Smith's, back in King Street. The shop on the left of the image was at the time of the picture occupied by Richmond the baker. In Bank Place are the premises of Neilson & Son, tailors. Other branch post offices in the expanding town were established at Duke Street (1900-1967), Waterloo Street (1967-1974), Foregate (1974-2022); Knockinlaw, Riccarton, and elsewhere.

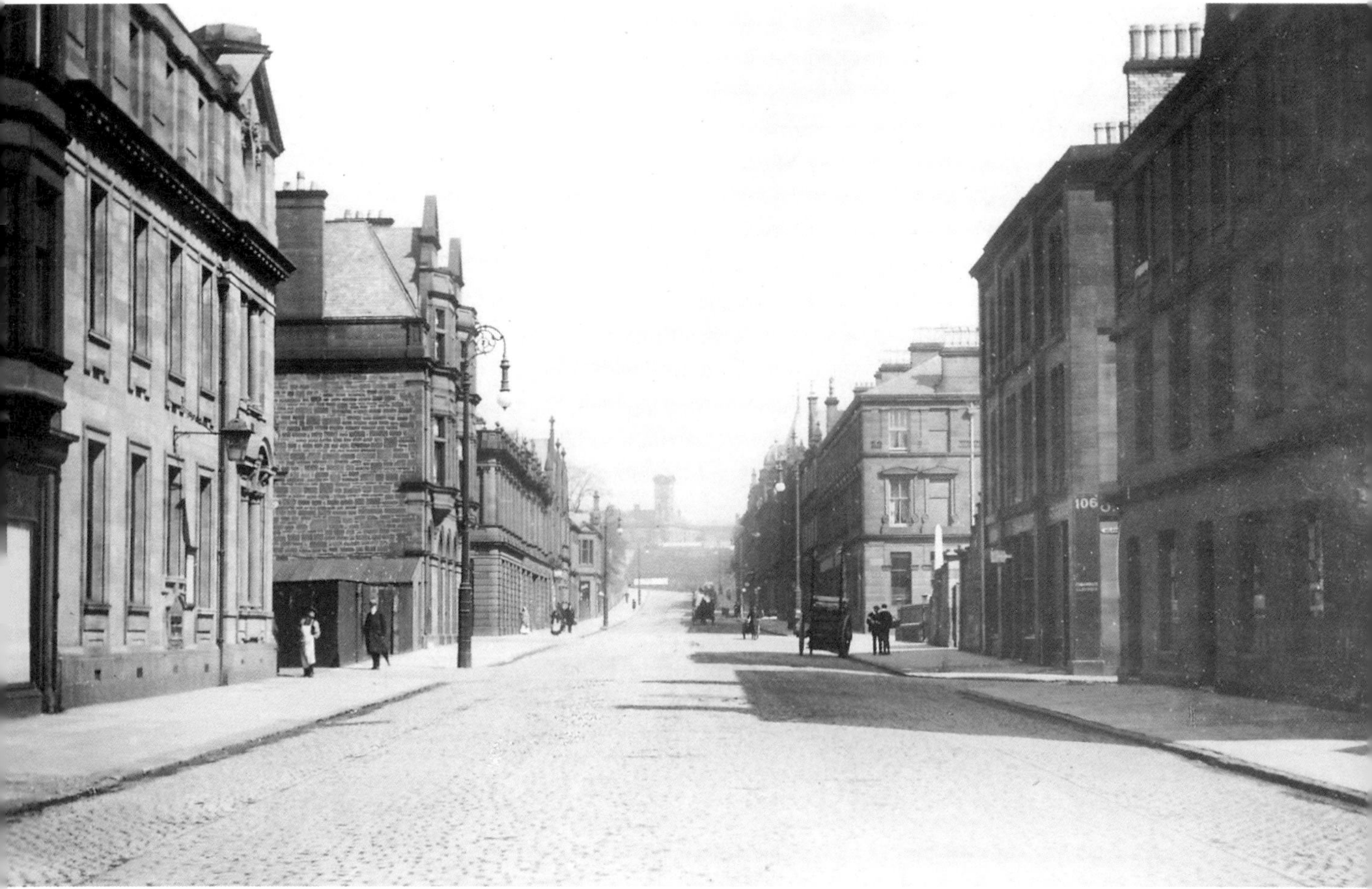
106

John Finnie Street South

The south end of John Finnie Street took longer to develop than the northern end. The buildings here date from the late 1800s, such as the former J. & J. Sturrock & Co.'s solicitors' offices, dated 1889, currently Pressure nightclub. On the immediate left, with the first and second floor bay windows, are the premises of George Tannahill & Sons, cabinetmakers and upholsterers. This is one of Kilmarnock's oldest firms, having been established in George Street in January 1882. The building was erected around 1895. Next door is the former post office building, erected in 1907. Beyond the post office is Nelson Street and a gap with some poorer standard buildings. A new block with a curved façade was built there around 1965 for the Halifax Building Society. The next building, with the arched windows on the ground floor and a decorative sandstone façade, was erected in 1890-91 for the British Linen Bank, from 1969 the Bank of Scotland. Beyond Grange Place is the long, low double-storey building with arched windows on the first floor and a balustrade on the eaves that housed the Savings Bank of Glasgow. It is now The Duke, a café bar. On the right-hand side, the first block was the Kilmarnock Arms, erected in 1899. Beyond Nelson Street is the three-storey building (numbered 106), which is Smith's Buildings. The gap beyond, which had some small buildings on it for a time, was redeveloped as the Royal Bank of Scotland, the modern concrete building being erected in 1972 to plans by Henry Dawes & Sons. At the far corner of Bank Place, the three-storey red sandstone building is the Royal Liver Assurance Office, erected in 1879-1880 to plans by William Railton. On the south-eastern corner with John Dickie Street is the Wallace Chambers, erected in 1905-06 for William Wallace & Co., one of Kilmarnock's major whisky producers, noted for its Real Mackay Whisky. The business was established in 1760 and ownership passed to the Mackays in 1878. It was taken over by Johnnie Walker in 1912. At the far end of the street the tower associated with Kilmarnock Railway Station is seen. This was built in 1877 following a redevelopment of the station buildings.

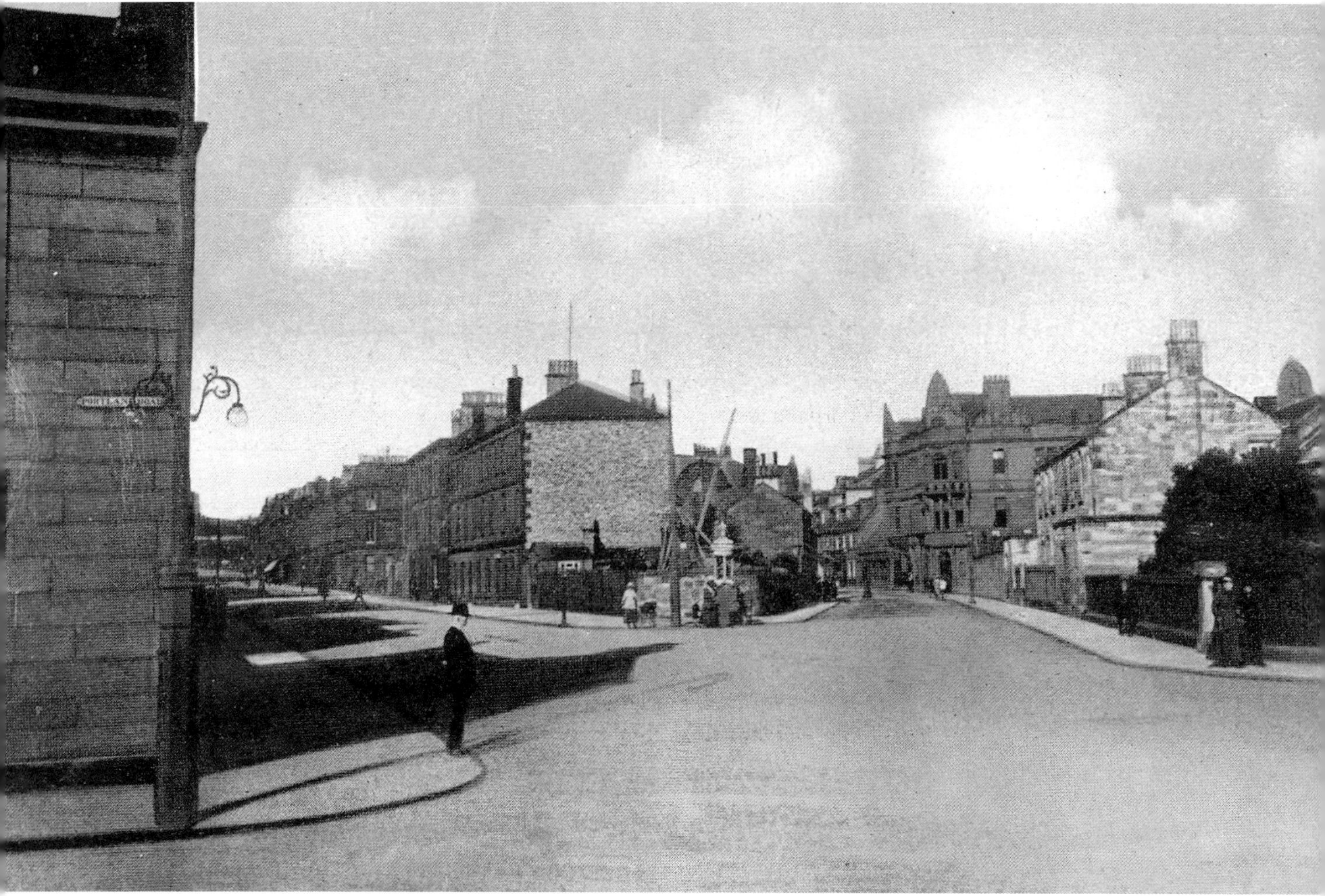

Bank Street

Bank Street is one of the older streets of Kilmarnock, linking Dundonald Road and the route south to The Cross, though the last short stretch is actually Cheapside Street. The streets predate the straight-line plan of John Finnie Street and Bank Place, which were imposed on it, resulting in the acute angular end of the street seen here, where it meets John Finnie Street, viewed from the Holy Trinity Church in Portland Road. The building on the left is 1 Portland Road, the street sign a giveaway. The brick gable is of the former Kilmarnock Arms inn, located in John Finnie Street, followed by Smith's Buildings, erected in 1876 by the Smith Brothers, manufacturing stationers and printers. The firm was established in 1819 and was noted latterly for printing whisky labels. Just beyond Smith's Buildings is the entrance to Nelson Street, another of the original streets hereabouts. The rest of the street beyond are the commercial premises of John Finnie Street. In the gusset between John Finnie Street and Bank Street one can see a builder's crane. At the junction of the street is the fountain erected in 1910 to mark the co-operative society golden jubilee. The decorative three storey building in the distance is located at the junction of Nelson and Bank streets, and is a red sandstone block dating from 1903-04, probably designed by Thomas Smellie. It was known as Caxton Chambers. The light-coloured building on the right is of Kilmarnock's Police Station, the constables being based there until 1978, when a new police station was erected in St Marnock Street. The original building had six cells within it, plus an additional triangular one built into the corner of an exterior boundary wall. There was a cook and wash house, and more elaborate Governors' Apartments. Behind the station was a walled garden, where prisoners could exercise, plus a passage leading to the Prisoner's Room in the Court House. An older gaol occupied the site. In 1888 'the telephonic system of communication' was introduced at Kilmarnock Constabulary Station. The railings to the right surround the former Sheriff Court House. The new court was erected in St Marnock Street in 1984-87.

A Look Back at KILMARNOCK ~ page 31

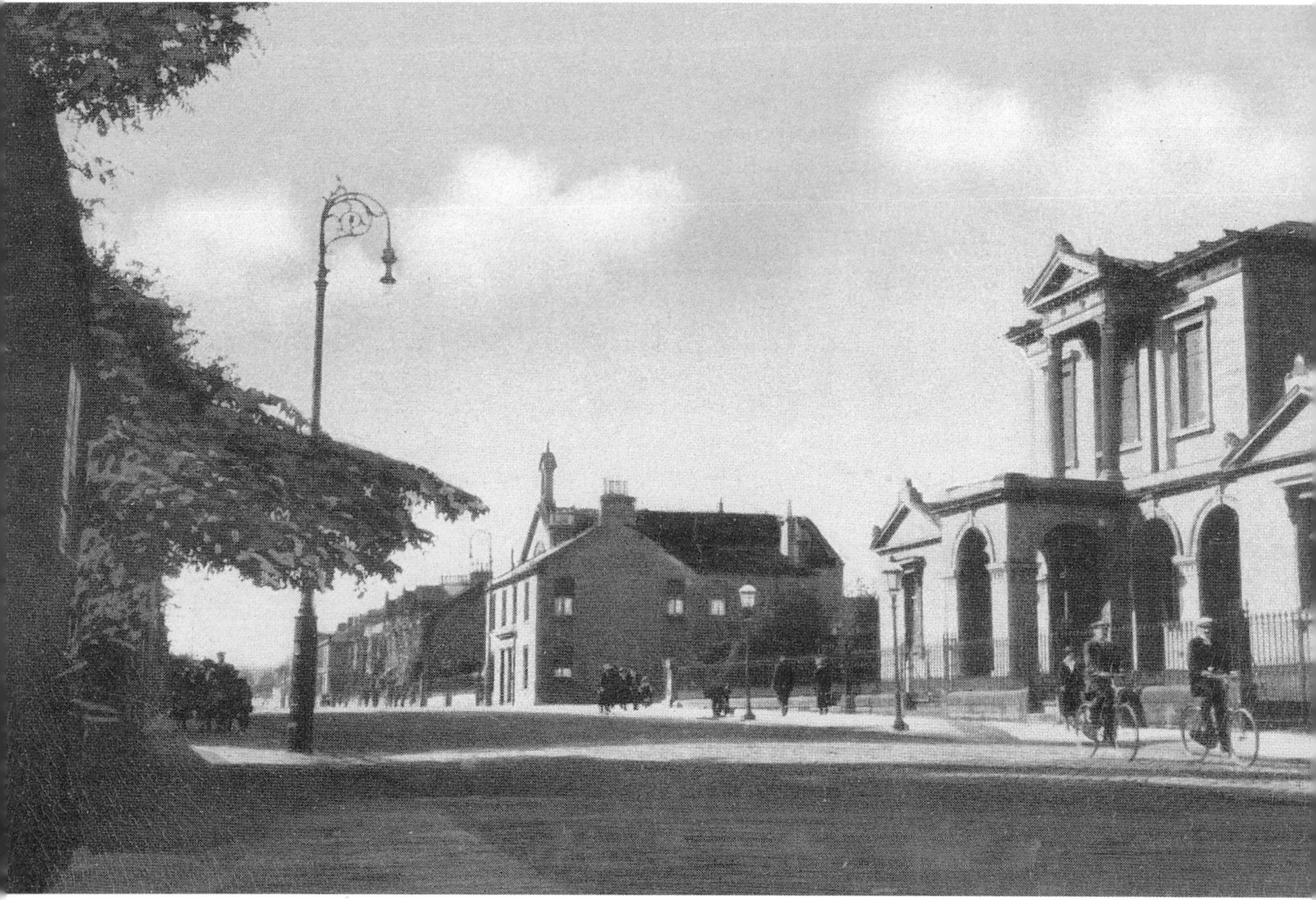

St Marnock Street

St Marnock Street extends westwards from King Street to the junction of John Finnie Street and Portland Road. The street was created around 1834, the bridge across the Kilmarnock Water at its eastern end being erected around then. Number 3 dates from 1859-60, designed by James Ingram; number 5 is dated 1868. On the right of the picture is the former Sheriff Court, erected in 1850-52 to the plans of William Railton. Internally, the court hall, which was almost square in plan, was located at the centre, and around it were the Sheriff Clerk's Rooms, Sheriff's Rooms, Jury Room, Procurator Fiscal's Rooms, Witness Rooms and a Kitchen. The smallest room on the ground floor was the Prisoner's Room! The first court held within the building took place on 5 May 1852, under the Sheriff, Thomas Anderson. He remained until he resigned in 1883. The building continued in use until a new court was opened across the road. The former court was then converted into the offices of the Procurator Fiscal. Beyond the John Finnie Street junction is the building at 1 Portland Road, currently a dental surgery. Behind it is the original Portland Road United Presbyterian Church. This was erected in 1859 to plans by the Edinburgh firm of Peddie & Kinnear. Built in a Byzantine style, it cost £1,900 to erect. In 1969-71 the church was demolished and a new, modern-style place of worship was erected on the same site. This was designed by Alexander Dunlop & Partners and was known as Howard St Andrews Church. It is now a church hall known as the Howard Centre for St Andrew's and St Marnock's Church. Beyond the church, Portland Road continues, originally the main road towards Irvine. On the south side of the street, but not in the picture, is St Marnock's Church, now St Andrew's and St Marnock's. Designed by James Ingram, it was erected in 1836 at a cost of £5,000. It had seats for 1,730. It was off this street that Kilmarnock House was located, an ancient mansion occupied by the Boyds, Earls of Kilmarnock, after Dean Castle was destroyed by fire in 1735. It dropped in status when it became a Ragged School until it was demolished in 1935.

Restaurant
GRAFTONS
Glass
GEORGE G. KIRK
REDMAYNE
YOUR TAILOR
W. WOOLWORTH & Co. Ltd.

King Street ~ Upper

King Street was built from The Cross southwards towards Riccarton, becoming Titchfield Street after the Fowlds Street junction. The street was created in 1804, at the same time as the New Bridge over the Kilmarnock Water was built. This view looks northwards towards The Cross from near Sandbed Lane, which strikes to the left towards Sandbed Street, the original old southbound highway from The Cross. The building on the immediate right was Cable's menswear shop, replacing one at 9 Regent Street. To the left of it was the narrow passageway known as Mitchell Street, even although it could only allow a single vehicle to pass along it. The premises of F. W. Woolworth follow, the original location of Kilmarnock's branch of the national chain. The next building was Grafton's, erected in the 1950s. The shop sold women's clothing. Market Lane follows. The rather grand stone building, with the three archways at ground floor level, was the National Bank of Scotland. David Lauder's Dining Rooms was located next door. Separated from Lauder's by Guard Lane was Kilmarnock's Town Hall. The Town Hall was erected in 1804-5, spanning the New Bridge, or King Street Bridge. The main hall was located on the first floor, with some shops located at street level. Also within was the Court Room, Superintendent of Police's Office and Town Clerk's Office. The building replaced the original Town House, which stood on the west side of The Cross, and which had a bell gifted to it by the Earl of Kilmarnock in 1711. From Guard Lane access was made to the police station, which had six cells. A couple of shops follow, before The Cross is reached. On the left of the picture is Hugh Lauder & Company Limited's shop, with the later restaurant that replaced the one on the other side of the street. This building dates from 1927, the work of Frederick Sage & Co, London-based architects. Lauder's was to be taken over as part of the House of Fraser chain of department stores in 1972, but it was closed around 2002. Most of the right-hand part of the street, apart from Grafton's, was demolished in the 1970s to allow the erection of new commercial premises.

A Look Back at KILMARNOCK ~ *page 35*

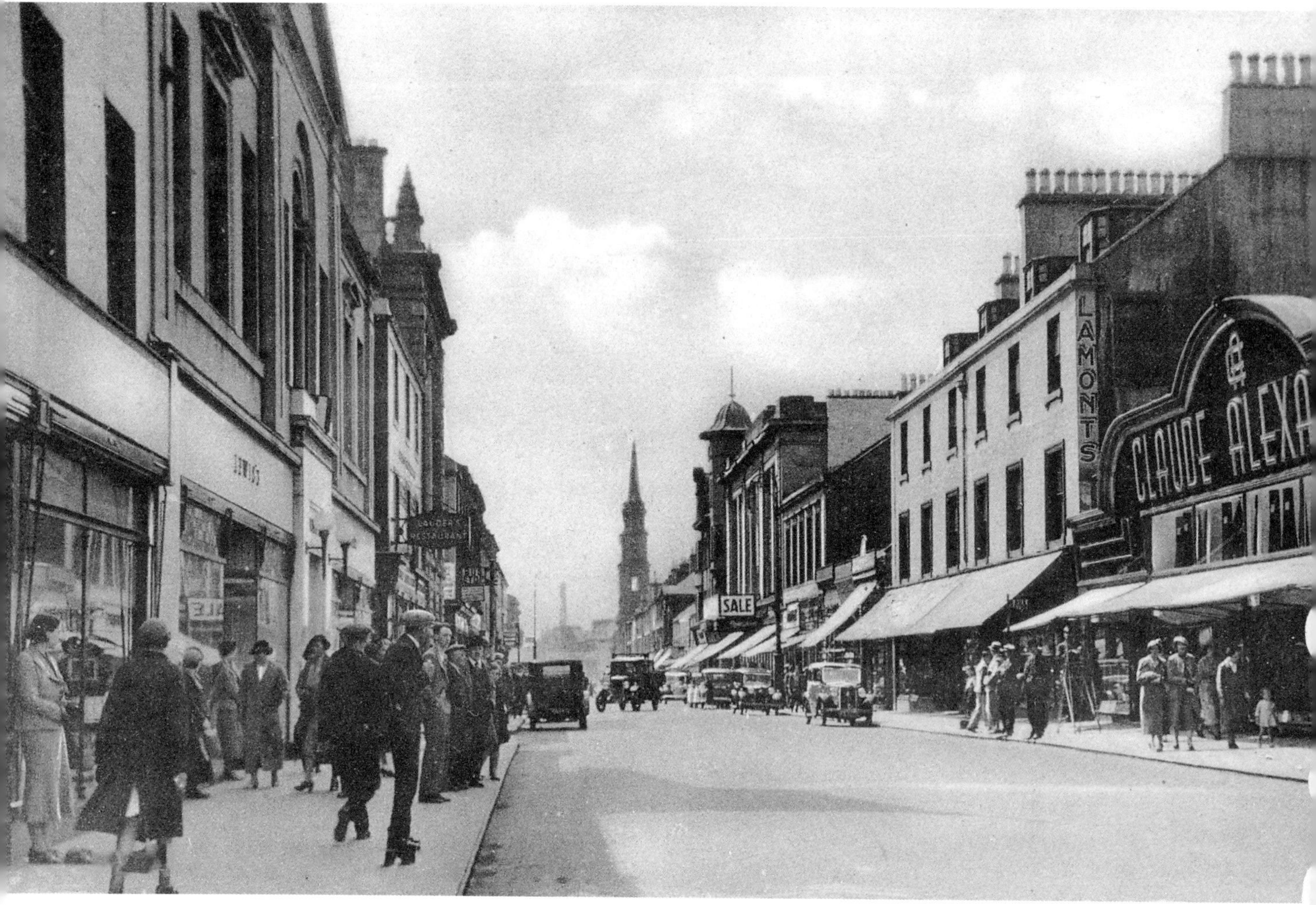
LAMONTS
CLAUDE ALEXA
SALE

King Street ~ Lower

This view depicts the middle stretch of King Street, looking south to the spire of King Street Church. On the right is Claude Alexander's tailors. This building stands over the Kilmarnock Water, which flows below King Street Bridge, unseen to shoppers in the pedestrianised roadway. Two bronze heads wearing swimming goggles are currently located on the pedestrianised roadway to hint at the water below. The Claude Alexander building was known as Victoria Place. Today the building is occupied by Claire's and Killie Gold. Lamont and Co. Ltd. was a tailors and outfitters. In the early 1900s their shop was located in the Wallace Chambers in John Finnie Street. This building was replaced in the 1960s by a white-tiled block, three storeys in height, and with three shops at street level. A narrow lane leads through to Sandbed Street, after which are some single-storey shops. In the 1950s, when this photograph was taken, these were occupied by the Buttercup Dairy, and Paige ladies' clothing shop. The double-storey building following was occupied by Robertson & Davidson's drapery and G. & W. Morton's shoe shop. This block was known as Morris Place, but it and the single-storey shops were redeveloped in 1987. The building is thought to have been named after James Morris, a local carrier who brought goods from Glasgow for over seventy years. The large sale sign is located on Lauder's department store. When it was taken over by the House of Fraser the name Fraser's was used, before it was closed and the shop subdivided. Beyond Sandbed Lane is the tall sandstone building with the distinctive corner tower and ogee-hatted lead roof. This was known as the Victoria Buildings, erected in 1901-02 to plans drawn up by Thomas Smellie. The building was erected for Robert Rogerson, the business being a grocery. On the left side of the street, Lewis's large department store occupied much of this end of the street, including the lower floors of the town hall. It was followed by Lauder's restaurant. Established in 1869, in the 1920s they were advertised as 'the most up-to-date tea rooms in Ayrshire'. The tall chimney located centrally at the end of King Street belongs to the Nursery Mills.

A Look Back at KILMARNOCK ~ page 37

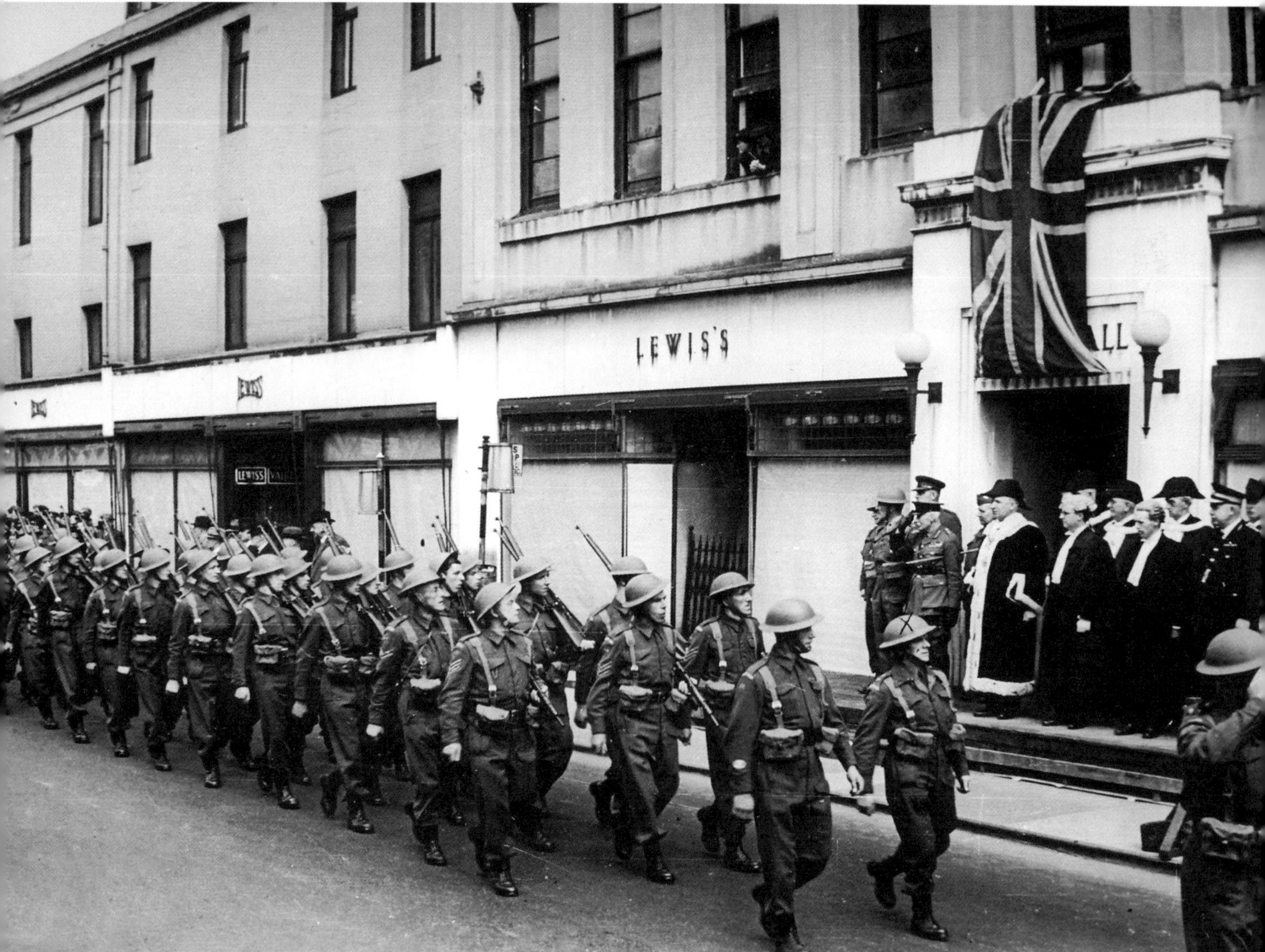
LEWIS'S

Second World War

During the Second World War a local battalion of the Home Guard was established in Kilmarnock to help protect the town in time of need. This photograph shows a parade of the Irvine platoon Home Guard making its way along King Street, passing the dignitaries of the town standing on the steps of the entrance to Lewis's Food Hall. Awaiting the salute is the provost of the town at the time, George H. Wilson. This took place in May 1943. The Kilmarnock guard was referred to as the 4th North Kyle Home Guard, and its men were drawn from Kilmarnock, Galston, Newmilns, Darvel, Hurlford, Fenwick and Craigie. The battalion was commanded by Lieutenant-Colonel D. M. Wilkie, with F. Richmond Paton of Hareshawmuir as second in command and Major Hugh B. Farrar as adjutant. In October 1940 one of the Home Guard Reviews held in the town had the men marching behind the pipe band of the Kilmarnock Academy Cadet Corps from the Cross as far as the main entrance to Caprington Castle, on the Ayr Road. Colonel Wallace Cuninghame of Caprington served as the Officer Commanding the Ayrshire Area of the Home Guard. In June 1942 King George VI visited Kilmarnock and reviewed the Civil Defence Services in the Howard Park. Kilmarnock played a considerable part in the war effort. The BMK factory swapped carpet-making for manufacturing shells. Glenfield & Kennedy made components for anti-tank guns as well as many other war-related engineering works, such as valves for Mulberry harbours. Local mansions were requisitioned, such as Bellfield House which became a base for training Special Air Service personnel, who also used Kilmarnock Baths. The power station cooling towers were painted in camouflage to try to prevent them from being a sitting target for German bombers. There was one air raid that affected the town, and four people were killed. In the early hours of Tuesday 6 May 1943, the Luftwaffe dropped fourteen bombs in a line from South Dean farm to the cemetery. The 50 kg bomb number 13 landed on a block of four houses at Culzean Crescent killing Janet MacGeachie, Alice MacGeachie, John Bissett and Dorothy Armour. Two of the houses were destroyed. At the end of the war additional names were added to the War Memorial in Elmbank Avenue.

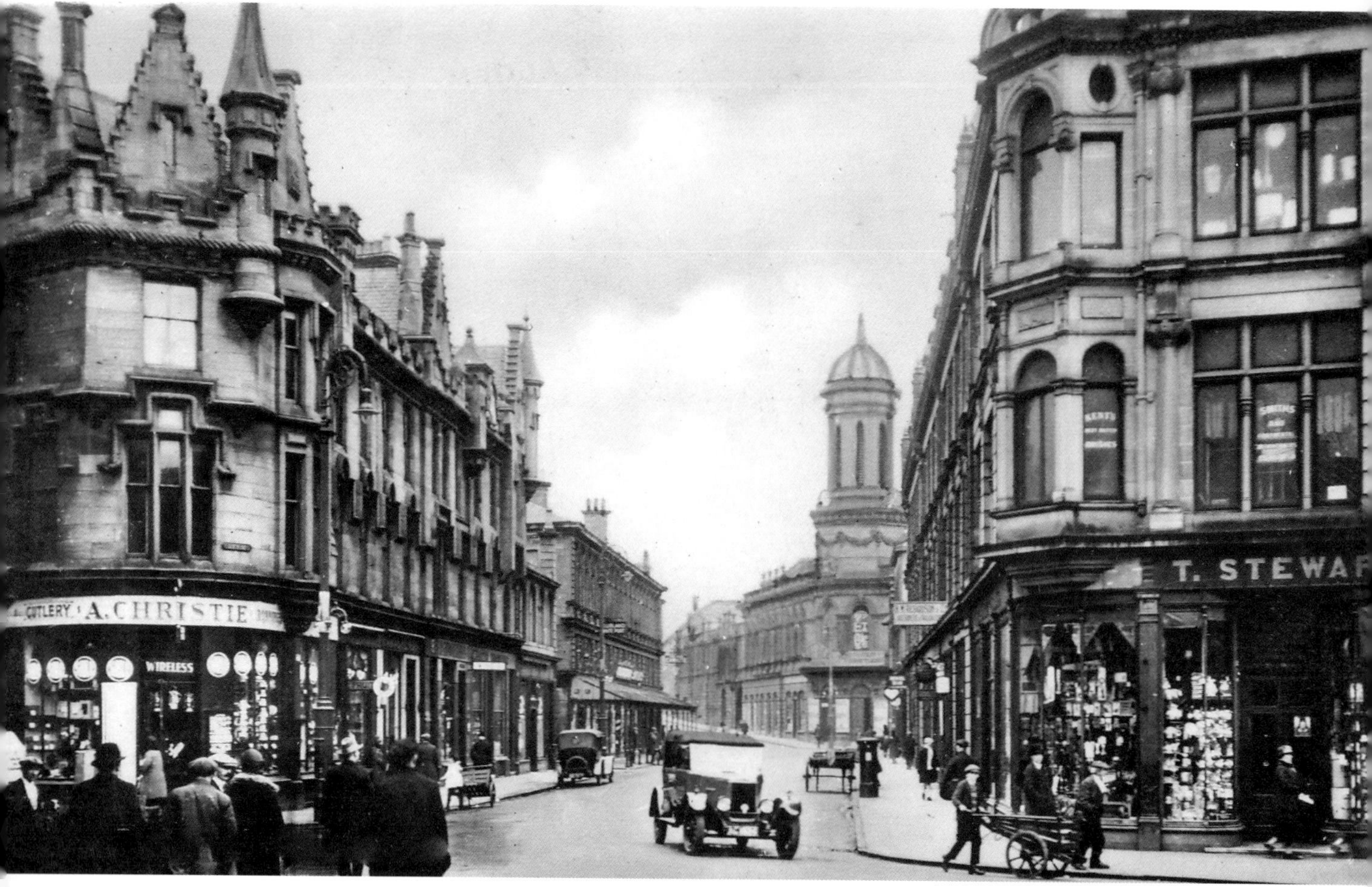
CUTLERY
A. CHRISTIE
WIRELESS
T. STEWAR

Duke Street

Duke Street was at one time one of Kilmarnock's most impressive thoroughfares. It extended from The Cross towards London Road. Before the street was cut through, the site was occupied by Nailer's Close and David's Lane, narrow roads heavily built-up with houses, tenements and a few smithies. Previously, traffic entering the town along London Road would arrive at Green Street and need to turn left, then right along the narrow Waterloo Street to reach The Cross. The idea for a new wider and direct route was that of the Town Improvement Trust and the architect of the street itself is thought to have been William Railton, of Kilmarnock, although many of the buildings within it may have been by other hands. The street was officially opened on 25 November 1859, when Provost Archibald Finnie and other civic dignitaries walked along it, followed by many of the town's inhabitants. On that morning there were no plans for any ceremony. However, the councillors decided that something should be done to mark the event, so the provost, magistrates, town council, Commissioners of Police and trustees for the improvement of the town assembled in the town hall, from where they marched in a procession to The Cross. They then walked the length of the new street to Green Street, before turning back to the Cross. There the Provost thanked everyone for accompanying him, and he publicly named the street after the Duke of Portland, who was given three cheers. Originally the street was to be named Victoria Street. Back at the town hall the dignitaries toasted the new street with champagne. The shop on the left was from at least 1869 occupied by A. Christie, ironmongers. The premises on the right facing The Cross belonged to Thomas Stewart and Son, ironmongers, and it included a new Royal Hotel. The projecting sign marks the office of H. M. Richardson, auctioneers and valuators, which operated in the 1920s. When the new one-way system was created, all of Duke Street was demolished and on its site the Burns Mall shopping centre was erected. The line of Duke Street remained through the centre of the shopping centre, linking the pedestrian underpass at the Palace Theatre with The Cross. Burns Mall was created in 1974-80 to plans by Hay Steel MacFarlane & Associates.

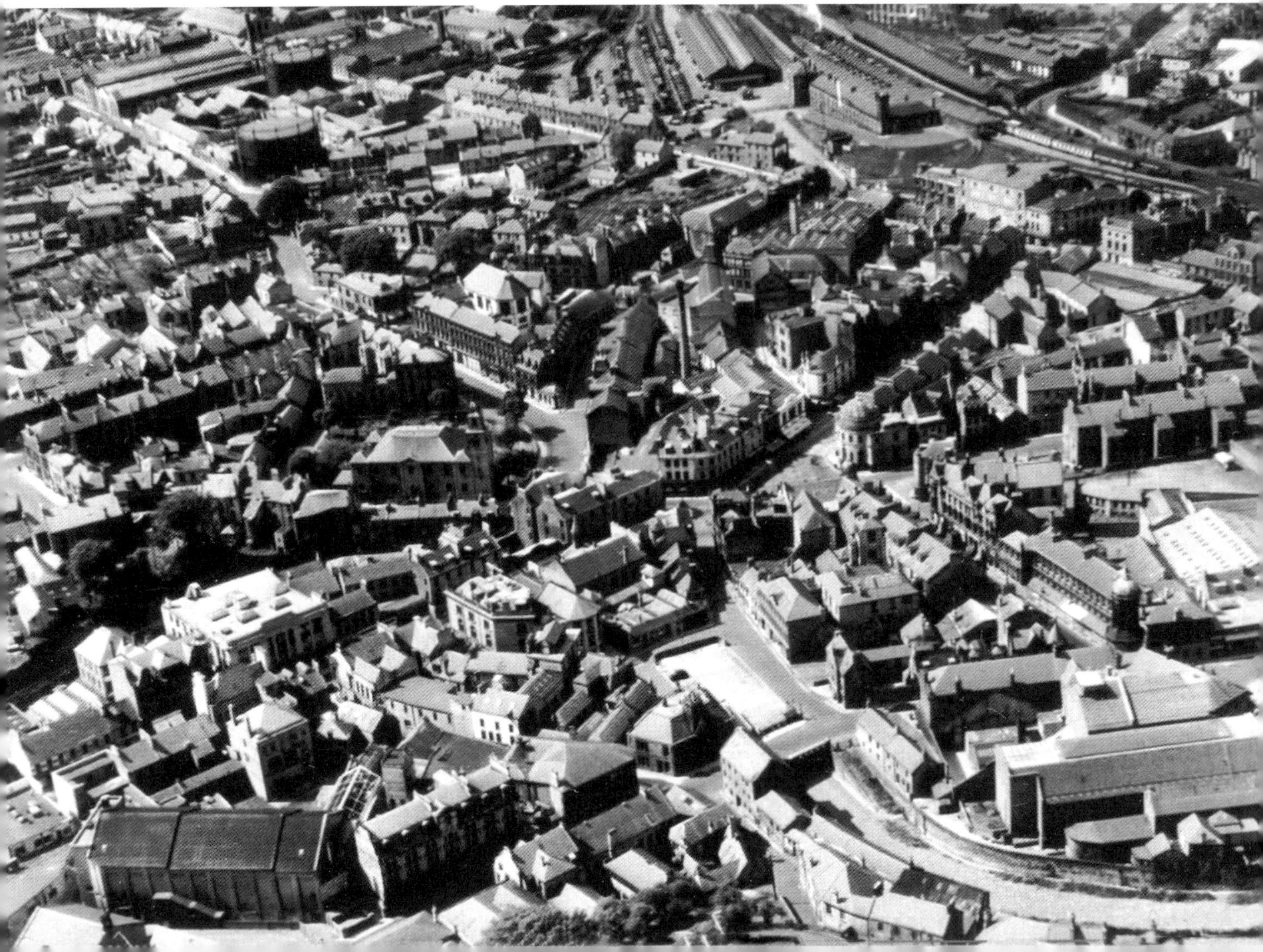

The Town Centre

This aerial view shows the town centre around 1950. Looking in a north-westerly direction, the photographer appears to have been in an aeroplane approximately over the academy in Elmbank Drive. People with a good knowledge of older Kilmarnock will be able to identify various buildings in the picture, as well as the old street layout. On the bottom right is the Palace Theatre (with the tower) and the Grand Hall. Above it is the former Duke Street, and to its right the light-coloured roof belongs to the old carpet factory, latterly Dick Brothers' garage. The old tenement houses in Foregate (or Fore Street as it was still known) can be seen, with the older and lesser houses of Clerk's Lane in front. To the left of the station sheds can be seen the long terrace of houses in West Langlands Street, and to the top left are the two gasometers of the gasworks. Kilmarnock's first gasworks was established in 1822 by the Kilmarnock Gas Light Company. This was taken over by Kilmarnock Corporation in 1871. Just visible in the top left is Morton's observatory – erected in 1818 by Thomas Morton but demolished in 1958. The line of Park Street and John Dickie Street leads one back down to the Laigh Kirk, just left of centre, and just above the centre of the image is the tall chimney associated with Johnnie Walker's premises. The Kilmarnock Water sweeps in from the bottom right, passing under the bridge at the old police chambers. These had been erected in 1898 to plans by Walter W. Reid, a Kilmarnock architect. The station was closed in 1954 but it remained as offices until 1972 and was demolished in 1973. To the right of this is the car park constructed over the Kilmarnock Water, part of Market Bridge, leading to Waterloo Street, and Mitchell Street extends from the police chambers towards the light-coloured flat-roofed building which is Lauder's department store in King Street. This was erected in 1927 to replace an older building destroyed by fire on 10 February 1923, causing £100,000 worth of damage. At the bottom left of the image is the large Plaza Cinema, opened in 1939, initially erected in 1937 as the Cuban Cinema.

A Look Back at KILMARNOCK ~ *page 43*

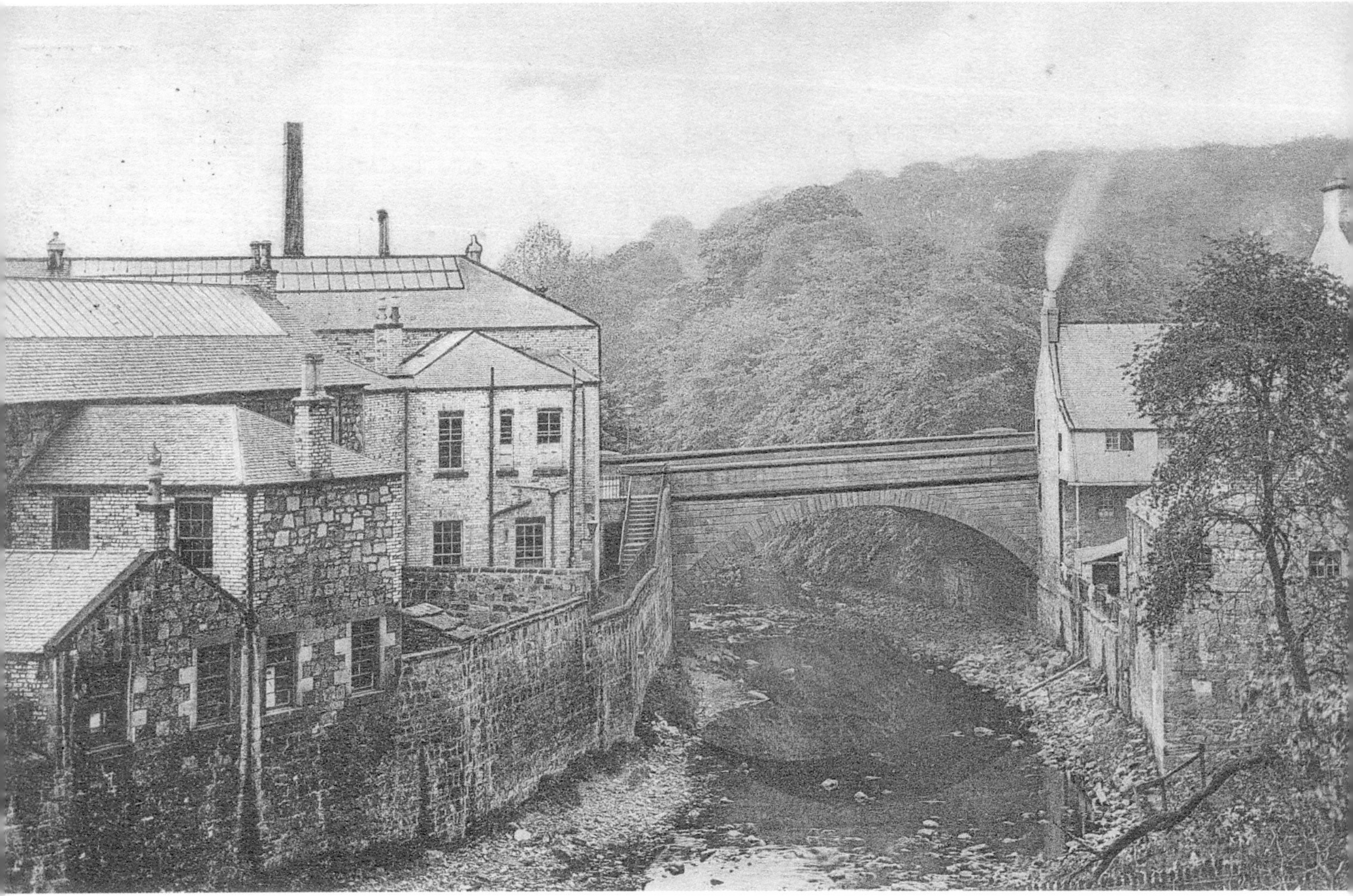

Green Bridge

The Green Bridge was originally erected over the Kilmarnock Water in 1759. It was not green in colour, but instead was named after the Town's Green, a public open space between Green Street and the river, used for public events and airing clothes. Before Green Bridge was erected, there was a ford here, but when the river was in spate it caused some difficulty for travellers heading east from the town. When the bridge was built the road splitting the green was created. A second bridge on the same spot was erected in 1827. The photographer is standing at Tankardhall Brae, a lane that links the old Braefoot with Braeside. This route was the original way into Kilmarnock from Edinburgh and Dumfries, but the steep brae caused issues, hence the new route becoming popular. The buildings on the left, or town side of the picture, formed part of the extensive burgh halls complex, buildings that were erected on the site of the old Kilmarnock Academy. The school had been erected on the old Low Green in 1808 to plans by Robert Johnstone. The playground was located west and north of the academy building. Adjoining the playground, next to Green Street, were the old Fish Market, Butter Market and Weigh House, with the Weighhouse Inn adjoining. Outside the Weigh House was the Weighing Machine, located on the roadway of Green Street. The Flesh Market was located behind the Town Hall, built over the river at the Fleshmarket Bridge. In 1862-63 much of the old academy was demolished and the new Agricultural Hall was built, as seen here, the building with the rooflights nearest the photographer, designed by James Ingram, with the 1885 art gallery building being behind it. In 1925 the halls were converted to the Grand Hall and the Palace Theatre was opened in 1903. The tall chimney is probably that associated with the carpet factory building which was located between the river and Green Street, at the far end of the High Green, simply called the Town's Green, or Kilmarnock Green after the Low Green was built over. The carpet weaving factory was probably Kilmarnock's oldest, and was operated by Messrs Gregory, Thomson & Co. The buildings on the right of the bridge were in London Road, but were demolished by the 1930s.

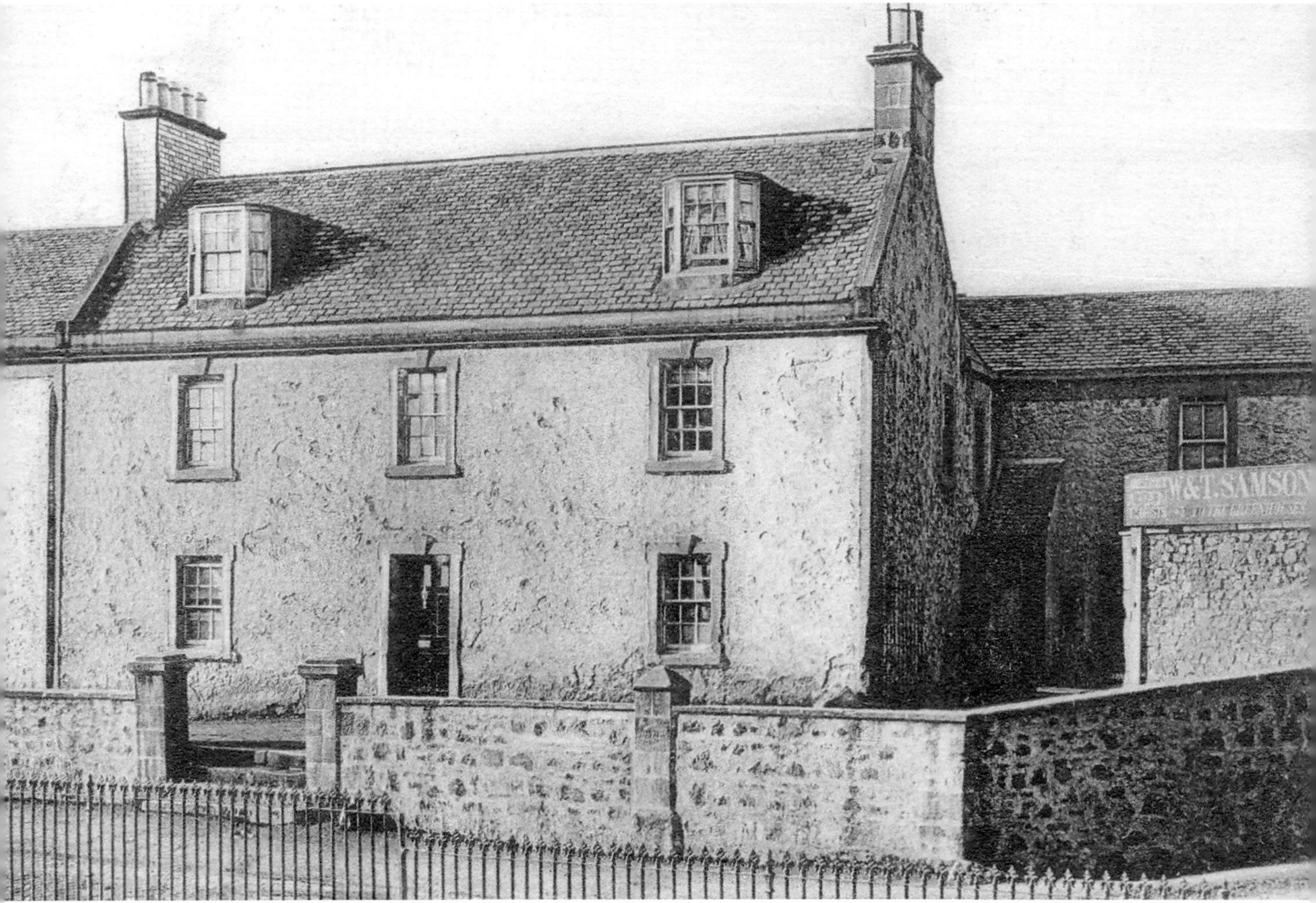
W&T. SAMSON

Robert Burns and Kilmarnock

Robert Burns has a number of associations with Kilmarnock, the most notable being the fact that his first book of verses, *Poems: Chiefly in the Scottish Dialect*, was printed by John Wilson at his press in the Star Inn Close, off Waterloo Street, although recent research has claimed that the printworks was located elsewhere. The book, known as the Kilmarnock Edition and now worth thousands of pounds, was printed on 31 July 1786, the 612 copies being sold within a month. To mark Burns' association with the town, a statue of Burns and Wilson was commissioned for The Cross and was unveiled by the Princess Royal on 27 September 1995. It was sculpted by Alexander Stoddart and also contains heads of Apollo and Hermes, representing poetry and trade. An older stone plaque that formerly marked the site of Wilson's printing works is located within the doorway of the Burns Mall. On 9 August 1879 a large memorial building, containing a museum of artefacts, was opened in the Kay Park, having been designed by Robert Ingram. It cost £2,893. This contained a marble statue by W. G. Stevenson, and a tower containing rooms that could be visited. The museum closed and was about to be restored when it was set on fire on 20 November 2004 and much of it collapsed. It was partially rebuilt and the Burns Monument Centre was built around it, creating a heritage centre and marriage suite. When Burns lived at Mossgiel, near Mauchline, he visited Kilmarnock fairly regularly, and he became acquaint with a number of residents. He refers to some of them in his poems, such as Rev James MacKinlay, Rev John Russell and Tam Samson. Burns was made an Honorary Member of the St John Kilmarnock Masonic Lodge, which originally met in the Commercial Inn in Croft Street. The bard's brother, Gilbert, was married to Jean, daughter of James Breckenridge, merchant in the town. This picture shows Rosebank, the home of Tam Samson, who was mentioned in Burns' *Tam Samson's Elegy*. He was a noted nurseryman. His house stood in London Road, next to Braeside. The house was demolished in the 1960s. A plaque marks the site and Samson's gravestone can be seen in the Laigh Kirkyard.

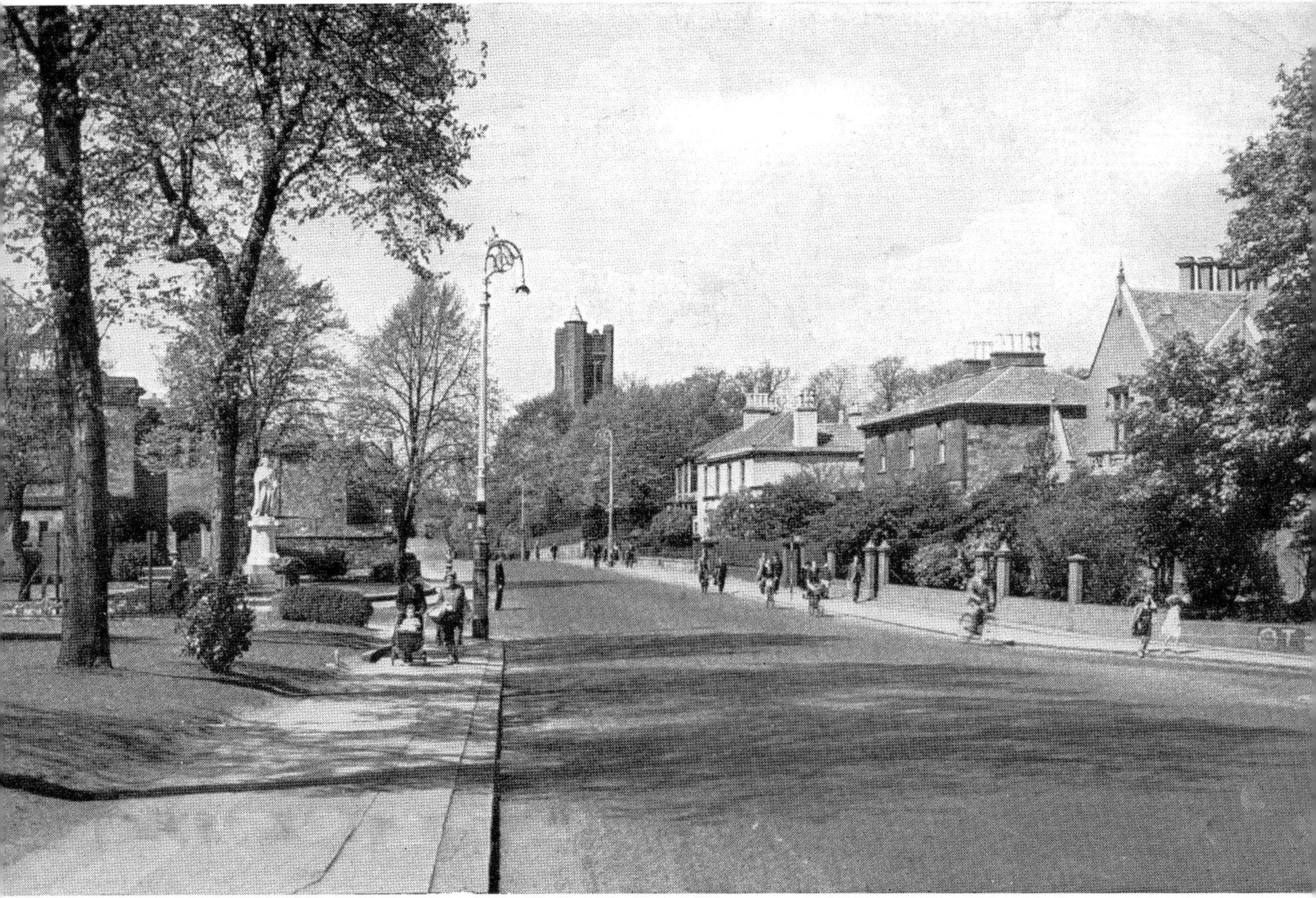

London Road

The road from Kilmarnock towards Edinburgh and Dumfries is rather grandly named London Road. It became one of the trendiest places to live in the town, and today still retains much of that grandeur, with large and imposing dwellings lining the street. This view is of the street from just outside the Dick Institute, looking back towards the town. The tower belongs to Henderson Parish Church, erected in 1907 to the plans of Thomas Smellie (1860-1938), author of *Sketches of Old Kilmarnock*, published in 1898. It was opened for worship on 8 September, the minister at the time being the popular Rev David Landsborough, hence the building often being referred to as 'Landsborough's kirk'. He is commemorated by a stained-glass window. Since 2012 it has been known as the Kay Park Parish Church, following a merger with the Old High Kirk. The Ravaccione marble statue is of Sir James Shaw (1764-1843), the Riccarton lad who went to make his fortune in London and ended up becoming Lord Mayor, serving from 1805-6. The statue, sculpted by James Fillans, originally stood in the centre of the roadway at The Cross, where it was unveiled on 4 August 1848, but in 1929 was removed here to aid traffic flow. To the left of the statue is the Masonic Hall belonging to the four lodges based in Kilmarnock. This was erected in 1926-27 to designs by William F. Valentine (1885-1957), a Kilmarnock architect who lived further along the road at number 21, known as Gardrum. The lodges are St John (erected in 1735); St Andrew (erected in 1771); St Clement (founded at Riccarton in 1768); and St Marnock (erected in 1767). Previously, there was a masonic hall in John Finnie Street. The buildings to the right of the image were houses forming 6-14 London Road. Numbers 6 and 8 form a semi-detached villa known as Annbank. Numbers 10 and 12 were used as surgeries. Number 14, with its gable left of the trees, was Abbey Cottage, at one time the home of James Donald, iron merchant. Immediately behind these houses stood Kilmarnock Technical College, from 1966 until it moved to a new site at Hill Street in 2016, though from 1 August 2013 it had been renamed Ayrshire College.

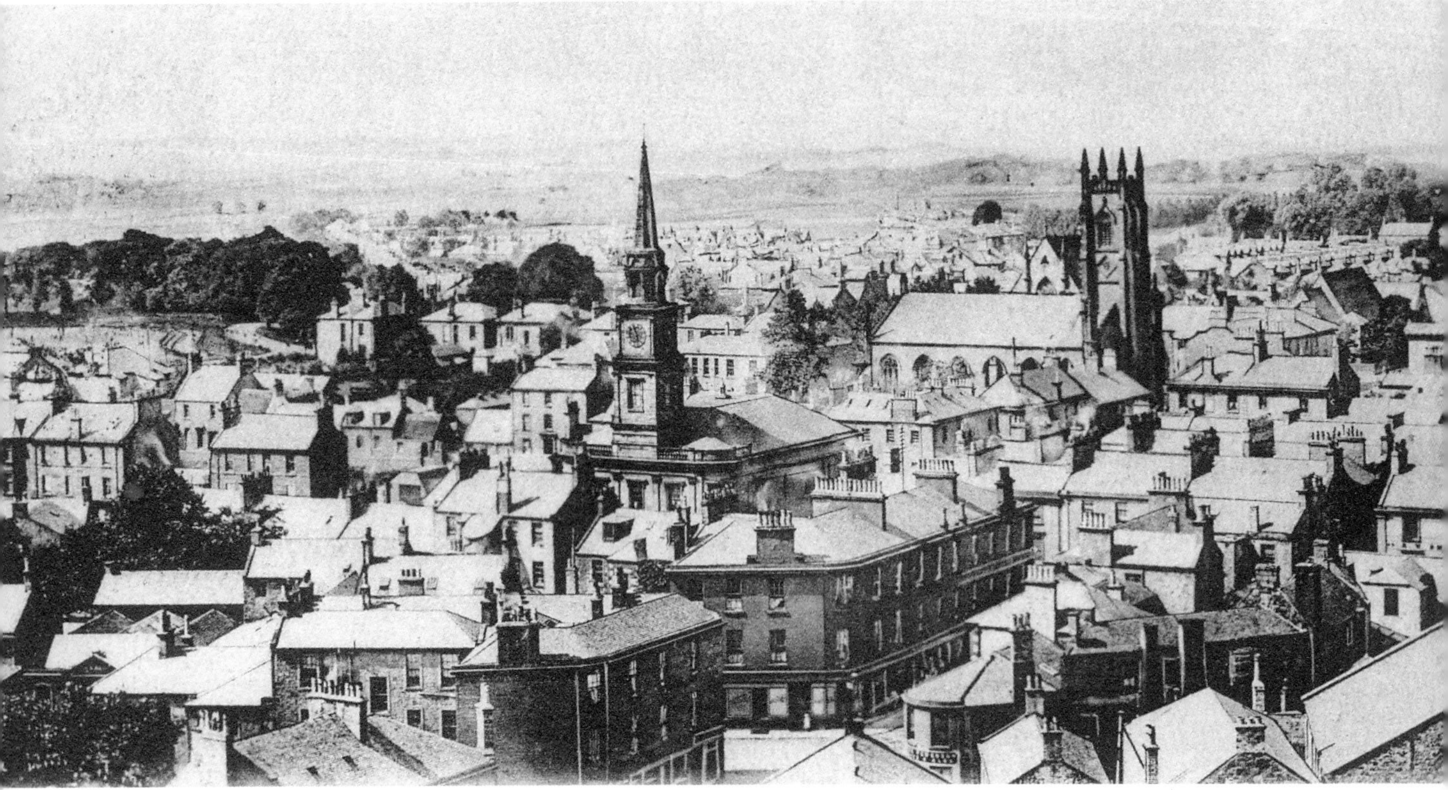

View from Academy

The hill on which the old Kilmarnock Academy stands is a notable viewpoint from where to gaze over the town centre. The steps up to the hill from Sturrock Street have been climbed hundreds of times by many of Kilmarnock's residents, as they made their way to and from the school. The view here is probably from the tower of the academy. Centrally placed in the image is King Street Church, and the square towered church is St Marnock's, erected in 1834-36 to the plans of James Ingram. To the right of King Street Church's tower can be seen Kilmarnock Grammar School, which was originally the Free School, and latterly Grammar Primary, until it closed in 1975. To the left of St Marnock's tower is part of the gable of the Winton Place Congregational Church, erected in 1860 to plans by James Ingram. The dark buildings in the foreground form the south side of Queen Street, linking King Street with Clark Street. It was named in honour of Queen Victoria. The round-fronted building was an inn, at the time the photograph was taken occupied by James Fergusson (1863-1903). The three-storey building between King Street and Princes Street had shops on the ground floor – amongst them being William Stewart's bakery. Between Princes Street and Mill Lane could be found Kelso's wallpaper shop. Most of the buildings in Queen Street were demolished and the King Street end rebuilt with modern shops. In the foreground, the four roofs were, left to right, of the Temperance Hall (formerly the Independent Chapel, erected in 1826), two other buildings, then the Reformed Presbyterian Church, originally opened in May 1825. The churches faced onto Mill Lane. On the right of the photograph can be seen A. W. Smith's premises in King Street. Other individual buildings can be identified – facing King Street Church, with the curved stair projection to the rear, was the Grosvenor Inn. For a short period, James MacKie had his printing business here – he produced a number of local books in the 1850s. He published the *Kilmarnock Weekly Post* from 1856 until 1865, and the *Ayrshire Wreath*. He was one of the secretaries of the committee that arranged the erection of Burns' Monument. In 1848 he published Archibald MacKay's *History of Kilmarnock*.

A Look Back at KILMARNOCK ~ page 51

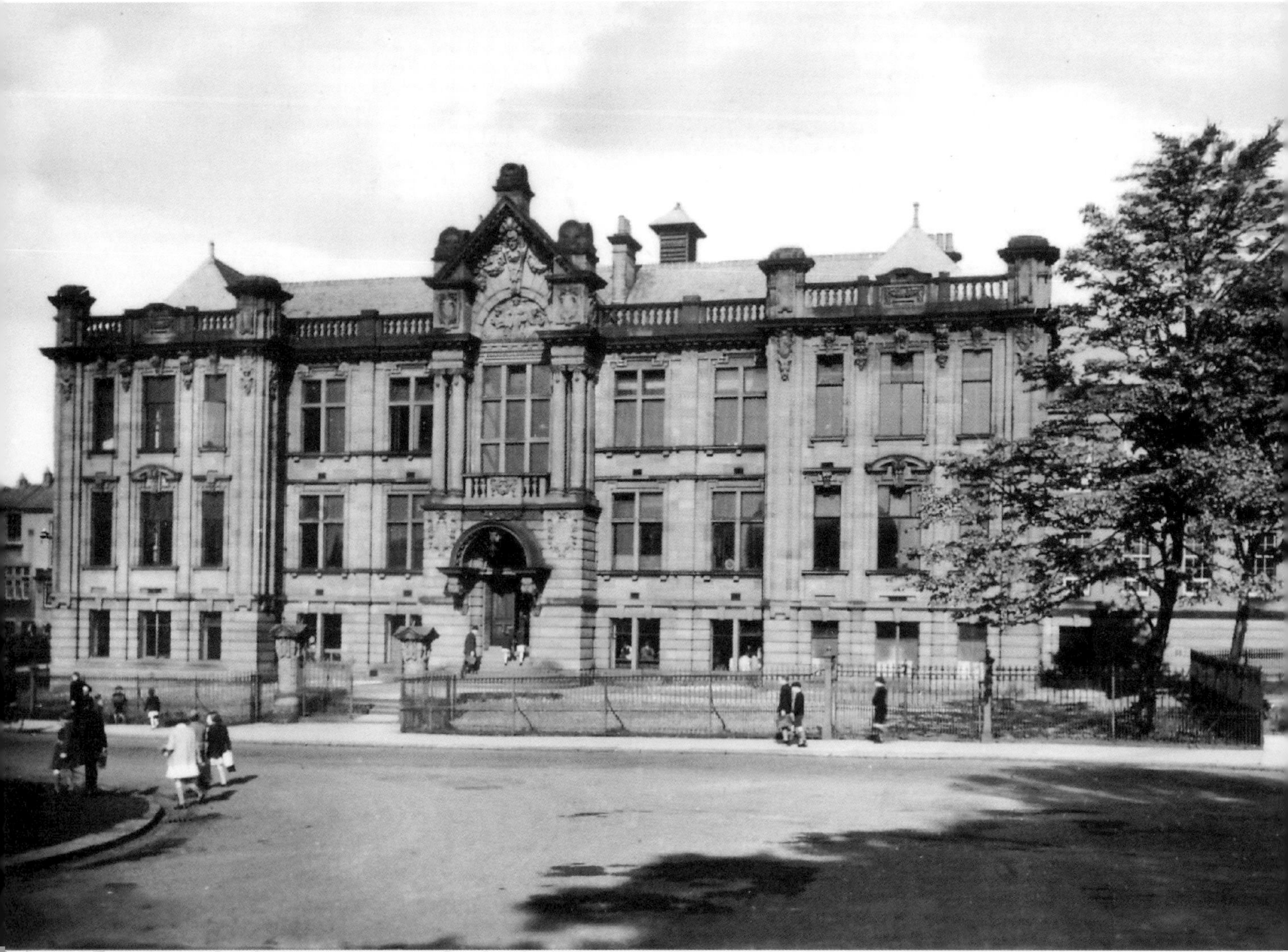

The Technical College

The Technical School, as it was originally known, was built at the bend in Elmbank Drive, next to Kilmarnock Academy. It was erected in 1908-09 to plans by Gabriel Andrew and was constructed using Ballochmyle sandstone. Some of the carved stonework have representations of science and art. The school cost £18,000 to build, some funds coming from the Scotch Education Board, but also from local subscriptions, including £500 from Miss Taylor, Kilmarnock, similar amounts from Lord Howard de Walden, and W. Baird & Co. Ltd, plus £875 from Andrew Carnegie. The building had 'laboratories for the study of chemistry, physics, mechanics, light engineering, heavy engineering, electrical engineering, hydraulics, mining, weaving, horticulture and biology.' In addition, students could study building drawing, art, domestic science, woodwork, metalwork and plumbing. Originally, it came under the control of the rector of the academy, but it was later to be separated and became the Technical College. The school was opened on 26 January 1910 by Lord Howard de Walden. Although a considerable building, the college was extended to the north in 1912, again in 1928, when the New Wing containing a gymnasium was built, and subsequently had to add an annexe, located in the former Glencairn School, and another in the former model lodging house in Soulis Street. The building was later to return to be part of an expanding Kilmarnock Academy, but in 1997 it was closed following a rearrangement of pupil catchment areas. Prior to the Technical School, an earlier school for teaching practical subjects had been established at Woodstock Street in 1878. Designed by William Railton, it cost around £1,550 to build. A brand-new technical college was erected at Holehouse Road. It was opened on 23 December 1966 by Rt Hon William Ross MP, Secretary of State for Scotland. The college was renamed Kilmarnock College, and in August 2013 was merged with Ayr College and the Kilwinning campus of James Watt College to form Ayrshire College. A new campus was erected at Hill Street, which opened in August 2016, the official ceremony being performed by First Minister, Nicola Sturgeon MSP. The Holehouse Road building was demolished in 2019 and replaced with private houses forming 'The Scholars'. The former Technical School was converted into residential flats in 2006.

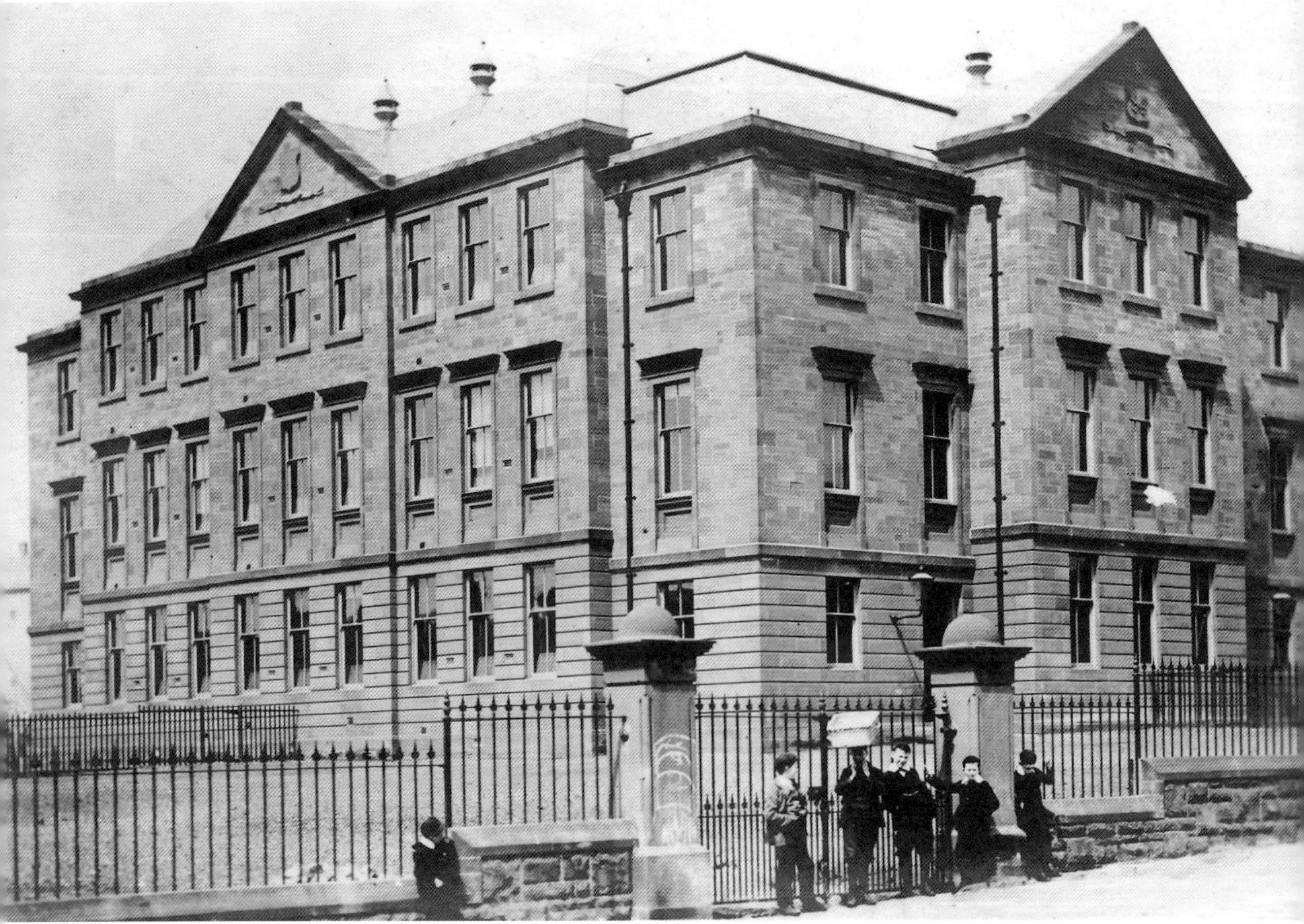

Loanhead School

Loanhead Public School was erected in 1903-05 to accommodate pupils in the eastern part of the town, where new housing had been erected over Tankardhall Gardens and around London Road. A plot between Dick Road and Loanhead Street was laid out, the tall sandstone building being centrally placed within it. The foundation stone was laid by the great philanthropist, Andrew Carnegie, on 29 August 1903, although the building was in an advanced state of construction. The architect of the building was Robert Ingram and he presented Andrew Carnegie with a trowel, spirit level and mallet so that he could perform the ceremony. A cavity was filled with items of interest from the time. On the same day, Carnegie was taken on a tour of the town by the council and he was also made a Freeman of the Burgh of Kilmarnock. The school was one of a number of schools where the younger children of the town were educated. Before the Education (Scotland) Act of 1872, schools were either operated by the churches, private individuals or parish councils. Loanhead was to be the seventh elementary school built by Kilmarnock School Board. It cost around £15,000 and was able to educated 1,000 pupils. Pre-Education Act schools in the town included King Street School (opened 1813), Free School in Dundonald Road (1817) Clark Street Academy, Female Industrial School (opened 1851), New Academy in Princes Street, Langlands Street School (opened 1845), Springvale Seminary in Dundonald Road, and East Shaw Street School (opened 1798). Other schools included Kay School (1869 – renamed Bentinck School); Wellington Street School (1869); the Grammar School; and Holm Mission School (1858). Roman Catholic children were educated at St Joseph's, built in College Wynd in 1865, but in 1903 it moved to a purpose-built building in Elmbank Drive, not far from Loanhead School. The secondary school, St Joseph's Academy, was relocated to a new building in Grassyards Road in 1956, the primary school which remained adopting the name St Columba's. As Kilmarnock expanded, newer schools were established in the various housing estates, including Shortlees Primary (1951); Mount Carmel Primary (1965); Annanhill Primary (1973); St Matthew's Primary (1973); Gargieston Primary (1975); Bellfield Primary; Silverwood Primary; Onthank Primary; Hillhead Primary; Kirkstyle Primary, and Whatriggs Primary (2019).

A Look Back at KILMARNOCK ~ *page 55*

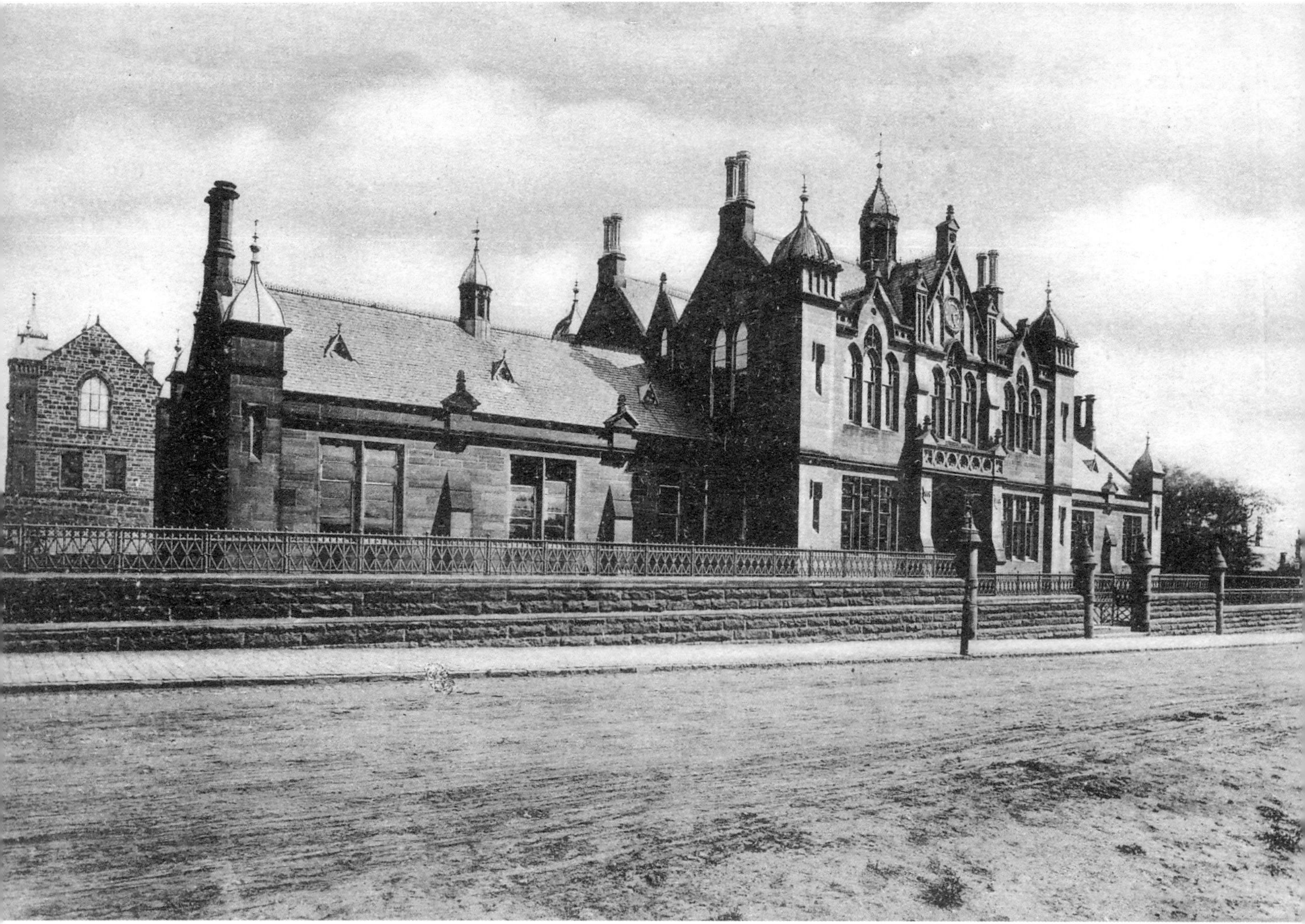

Old Kilmarnock Academy

When this building was opened it was the new Kilmarnock Academy, replacing the building at Green Street. The school was erected for Kilmarnock School Board (which had been established in 1872) to plans by William Railton (1820-1902). He was a Kilmarnock-based architect, and his interest in historical architecture is reflected in his contribution of plans of castles to MacGibbon and Ross's *Castellated and Domestic Architecture of Scotland*. The foundation stone was laid on 20 November 1875. The school cost £4,500 to erect, the work carried out by Andrew Calderwood, a local builder. The school opened to its first pupils in August 1876. At that time, it had 426 pupils on the roll. The school stood facing North Hamilton Street, between Woodstock Street and Old Irvine Road. The stone building with the arched window to the left was an addition of 1878, also by Railton, which housed the School of Science and Art. The first headmaster was Hugh Dickie. It was in this school that Sir Alexander Fleming, of penicillin fame, and Lord John Boyd Orr, of agriculture fame, were educated. The building, and its fairly cramped location, meant that the number of pupils wishing to attend soon outgrew the accommodation. A newer academy building was erected in 1898 at Elmbank Drive and the pupils were transferred there. When the new academy opened, this building was to become Hamilton Public School. The first headmaster was George A. Innes MBE, who remained for 25 years. He was noted as an amateur actor. Hamilton Public School was to be renamed Grange Junior Secondary School, following the opening of the James Hamilton Central School in 1933, named in honour of Rev James Hamilton, who had served as chairman of the Ayrshire Education Committee for years. The Grange school was relocated to a new building in Beech Avenue in August 1966, named Grange Academy, and it continued until 2008, when the new campus building was erected, incorporating Annanhill Primary School and Park School. The old academy site was then used as Woodstock School. The site is now occupied by the Flowerbank Early Childhood Centre and the Sir Alexander Fleming Centre, a facility for people with physical difficulties, opened on 17 March 2015.

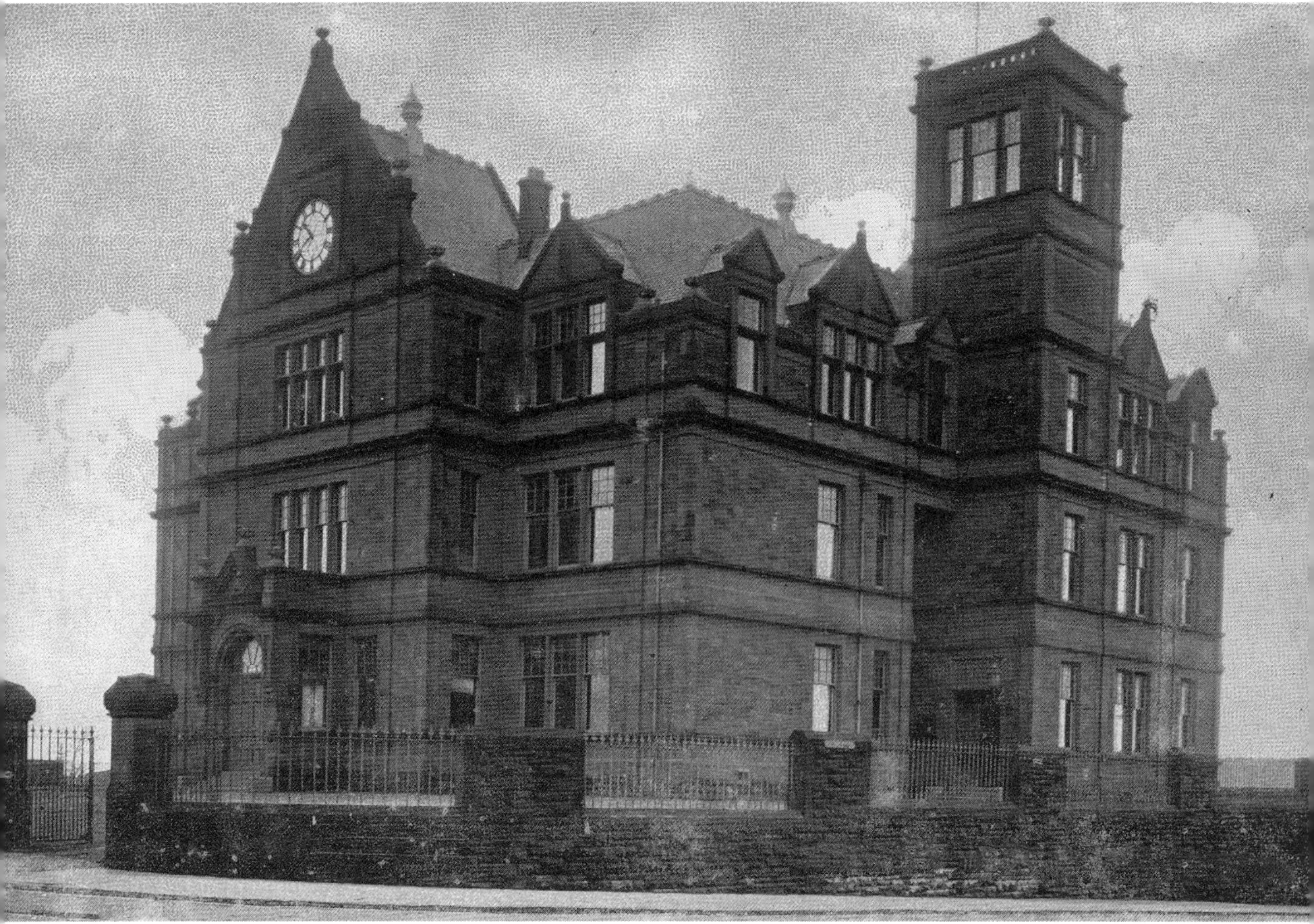

Kilmarnock Academy

The building shown here is the Kilmarnock Academy premises erected in 1898 to plans by Robert Ingram. The site chosen was originally a nursery, and two acres were used as the playground. The foundation stone was laid on 31 October 1896. The site also allowed room for expansion. Built of red sandstone, the new school contained a gym, swimming pool and workshops, in addition to the usual classrooms. A public clock faced the town centre, and a tall square tower, eighty feet in height, was originally used for astronomy lessons. There was accommodation for 868 scholars over the ground and second floors. The third floor had cookery rooms, a lecture room and a chemical laboratory. In total there were 22 class rooms and the school cost around £23,000. There was also a swimming bath, workshop and gymnasium. The school was opened on 12 September 1898 to pupils, but the official opening was held back until 9 February 1899 to allow all of the building to be completed. The opening was performed by Major General Sir Robert Murdoch Smith (1835-1900), a former pupil of the old academy, who found fame as an engineer and archaeologist. He was accompanied by James Thomson FGS, and both of them were awarded the Freedom of the Burgh. The first headmaster in the new building was Dr Hugh Dickie, the same man who was appointed headmaster of the previous academy. Described as 'the most outstanding teacher of his time' he retired in 1904. On 24 March 1923 the academy war memorial was dedicated by Sir Charles Fergusson of Kilkerran. It was designed by former pupil and local architect, W. F. Valentine. The second world war dead were commemorated by a new library, opened in 1955. The school had to be extended a few times – in 1946 the new dining block was built, in 1968-69 the Main Building, and in 1997 the Modern Technology Block. The academy continued to educate pupils until 29 March 2018 when it was replaced by a new Kilmarnock Academy, located in the William MacIlvanney Campus, New Farm Loch. The building shown here was acquired by Centrestage in 2019 and used as an arts academy. Centrestage was founded in James Little Street in 2006 by Fiona McKenzie and Paul Mathieson.

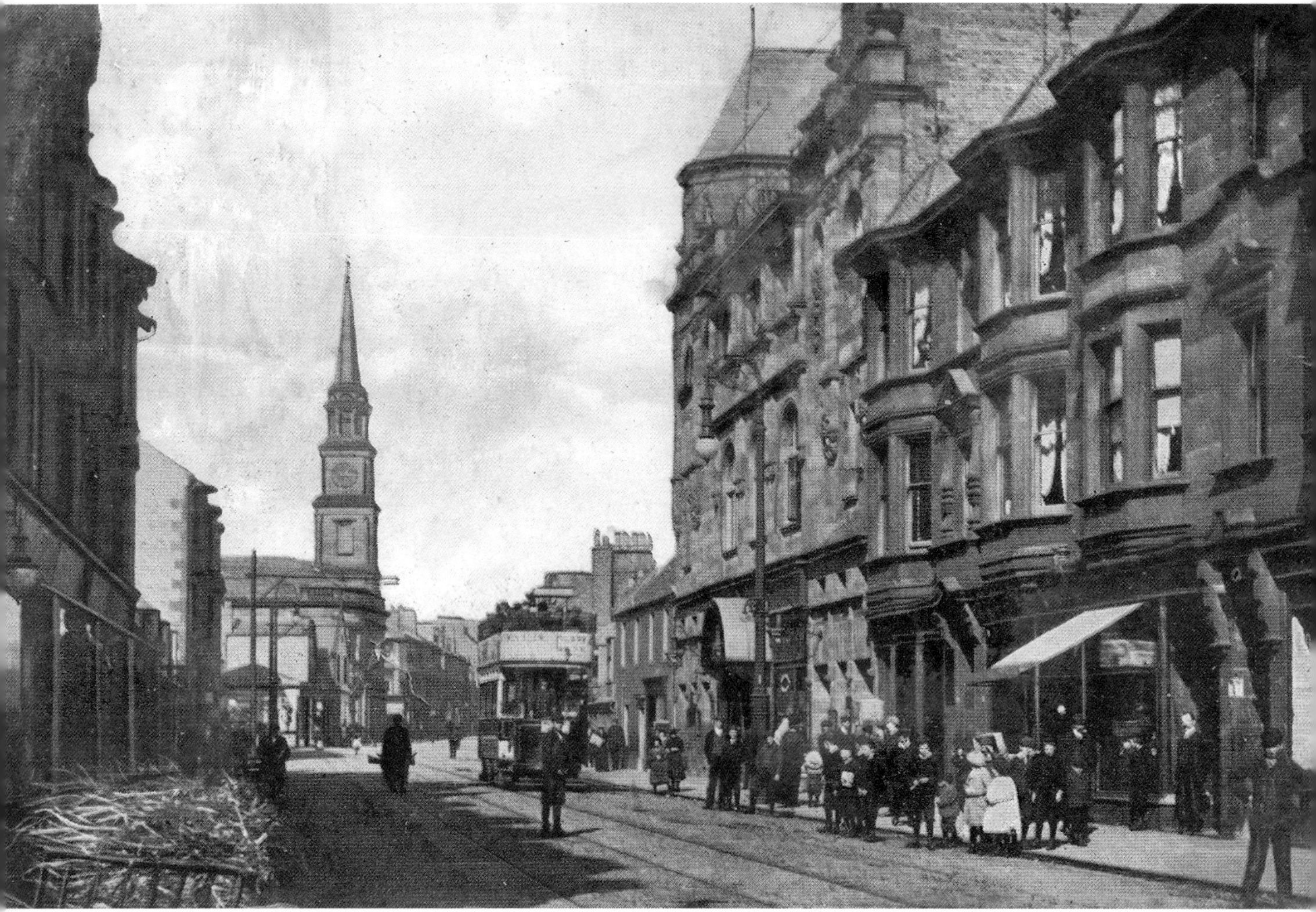

Titchfield Street

The continuation of King Street south of Fowlds Street junction is known as Titchfied Street. Like many of Kilmarnock's main roads, the name comes from one of the Duke of Portland's lesser titles – Marquis of Titchfield, taken from the name of one of his family seats – Titchfield Abbey. Titchfield Street was laid out from around 1765 as part of the Earl of Glencairn's development of the area, but in 1865 it was widened and straightened off and soon became one of the more important commercial parts of the town. The building on the right of this photograph is numbers 32-42, a three-storey red sandstone block with flats over shop premises. Next door was the King's Theatre, another red sandstone confection, highly decorated with three arched windows on the first floor, swags and pilasters, and two towers at roof level. The King's was erected to plans by Alexander Cullen and opened on 3 October 1904. It could seat 2,000 patrons, but the original owners failed after four years. The first 'talkies' in Ayrshire were shown here in 1929. It was latterly the Regal then ABC Cinema. Next door in the picture is a double-storey late eighteenth-century block, but this was later demolished and the Empire Cinema occupied the site. This, too, has been demolished and currently a modern double-storey block with false arched first-floor windows is located there. The tram in the image dates the picture to sometime between 1904 and 1926, the period when Kilmarnock Corporation Tramways operated. The 120-feet tall spire belongs to the King Street Church. This was erected in 1832 on the site of some older properties, designed by Robert Johnstone. The church was closed and the building demolished in 1966. On its site a steel and brick structure for shops was erected, but this too was removed in 2021, leaving an open plot. Titchfield Street continues south as far as Netherton Street. Within it were important buildings such as Kilmarnock Fire Station (opened 1937), designed by Gabriel Steel, replaced by a new one at Riccarton on 25 March 1994, and Kilmarnock Baths (1938-40), designed by Alexander Dunlop, with a pool 100 feet by 42 feet containing a unique wave-making machine, the first in Great Britain. The baths were replaced by the Galleon Centre in 1987.

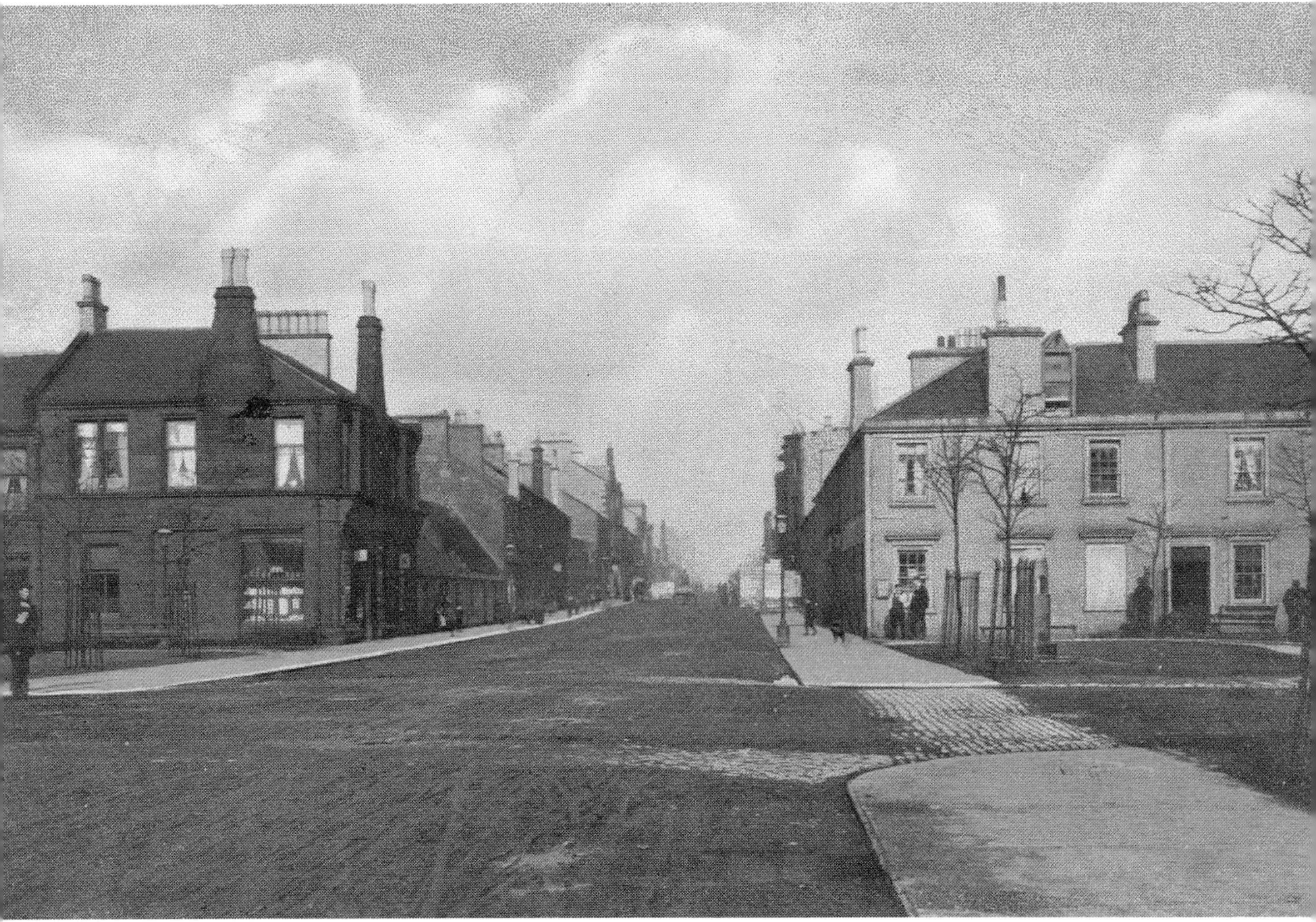

Glencairn Square

Glencairn Square was laid out at the bottom end of High Glencairn Street in 1765. Low Glencairn Street continues south from the square, and East and West Shaw Streets extend to either side of it. This part of Kilmarnock was a formally planned extension to the town, named Nethertown Feus, almost filling the land between the two rivers. Originally the square was referred to as Holm Square, but this gradually changed to Glencairn Square. The area became home to a number of industries, such as the Glenfield Print Works, later to be Glenfield & Kennedy; the Burnside Print Works, which became the Burnside carpet factory of BMK; and the Irvinebank Printworks, which became the site of the power station. In addition, there was a freestone quarry, the Glencairn Mill, and many nurseries and orchards. The first walk arranged by the Kilmarnock Glenfield Ramblers started at Holm Square, the members walking to Dundonald Castle. The club was formed in 1872 and survived until recent years. Originally a line of houses marked the edge of the square but after the Second World War the south-west and north-east corners were demolished, destroying the layout. This old view shows the end of South Glencairn Street. The building on the left was Glencairn Square Post Office. On the right-hand side are houses. Not seen in the image, but located on various sides of the square, were the Hunting Lodge Hotel and Howard Arms Inn. The Hunting Lodge occupies the site of two earlier inns. The present building was erected around 1930 to plans by William Valentine. In the north-east corner was the Salvation Army Hall. Just off the square, in West Shaw Street, was the Glencairn Church. It was erected in 1881 to plans by Robert Baldie as the Holm United Presbyterian Church, but became the Glencairn United Free Church. It was demolished in 1993. On the south-east side of the Square, and extending into Low Glencairn Street, was the No. 5 Branch of the Kilmarnock Equitable Co-operative Society. The buildings were erected in 1892 on the site of Alexander Gilmour's grocery. The co-op built three shops – a grocery, butcher's and sho shop, in addition to nine houses. The plans were prepared by Gabriel Andrew.

A Look Back at KILMARNOCK ~ *page 63*

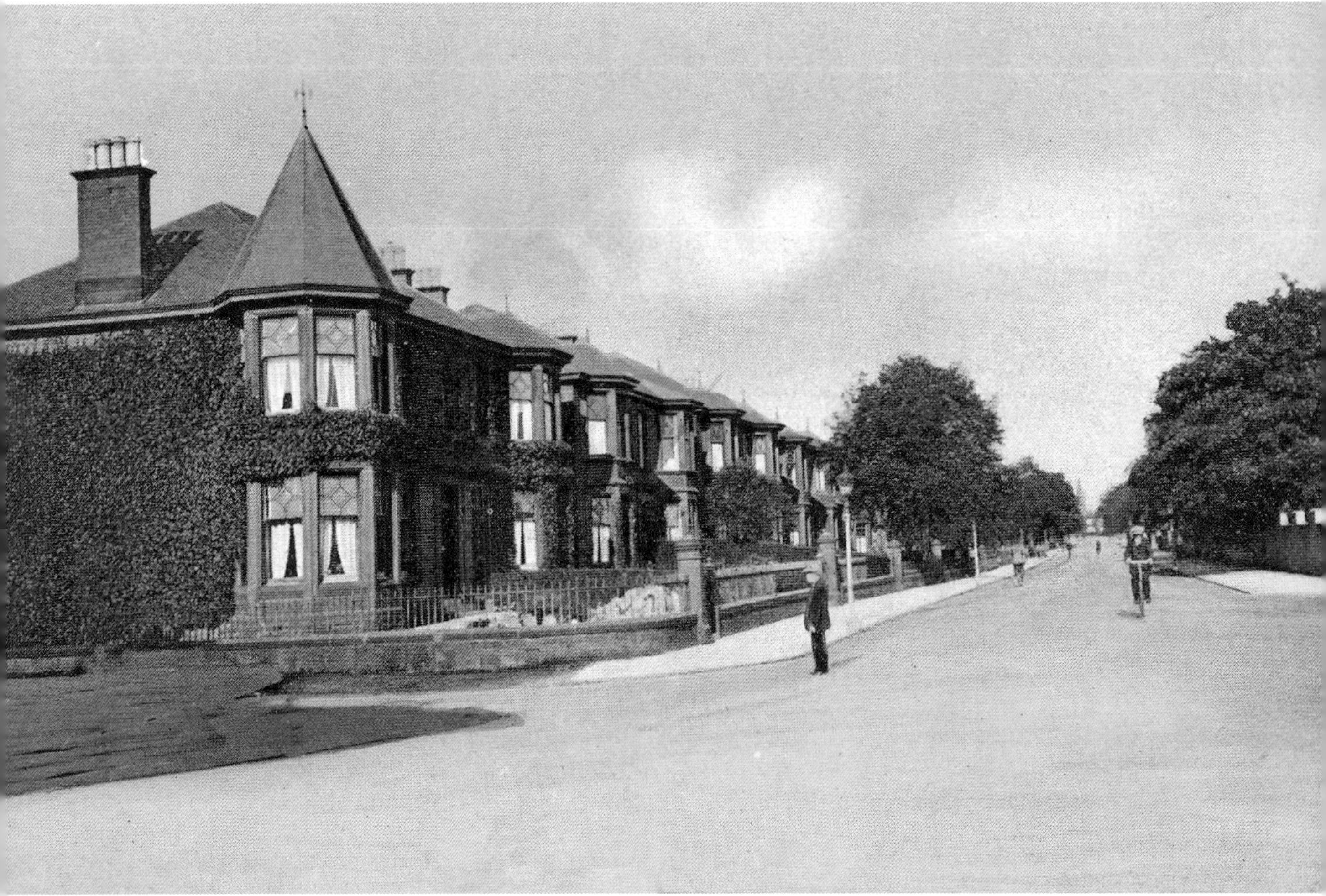

Dundonald Road

Many of Kilmarnock's businessmen erected large villas for themselves in the fashionable Dundonald Road. This image shows the line of semi-detached houses to the east of Dundonald Place, the corner house with the turret being number 99. The houses were erected soon after 1895 on what had been part of Westmoor Nursery. Kilmarnock had a fair number of nurseries around it, including Holmes Nursery, and Wards Nursery, both in Dundonald Road. On the right-hand side of the image, behind the wall, is Auchenheath (number 90), a rather fine arts and crafts house designed by James Hay and erected in 1909. On the same side of the street, number 82 was Kilmarnock Burgh Police's administrative headquarters from 1954. The burgh police station in Sturrock Street, which had opened in 1898, had become too small for all of the police's requirements. Kilmarnock Burgh Police amalgamated with Ayr Burgh Police and the Ayrshire Constabulary on 15 May 1968. In 1977 a new police station opened in St Marnock Street, resulting in the closure of this office. Number 101 was also designed by James Hay. Other houses in the road included Princes Street Church manse. Wards House was at one time situated in open countryside, but it was later subsumed into Dundonald Road. The older nineteenth century house was extended in red sandstone with a large bay window and side extension – it is now a doctor's surgery. Number 17 has an 'AS' monogram. The Springvale Seminary (at numbers 14-16) was a private school for girls operated by the Misses Young in the mid nineteenth century and then the Misses MacGlashan from 1866 until 1874. In a lane off Dundonald Road was the Free School, which was acquired by Kilmarnock School Board and converted into the Grammar School. In the mid nineteenth century the Cattle Market was located in Dundonald Road, at the spot where Wards Place and Beechwood Nursery is now. Many prominent Kilmarnock businessmen lived in Dundonald Road, such as Robert Blackwood (of Blackwood Brothers carpet manufacturers), and James Ingram (1799-1879), architect of many of the prominent buildings in the town. Dr Alexander Marshall (1827-1884) was another resident – after he died a large memorial was erected in his memory in the nearby Howard Park in 1896.

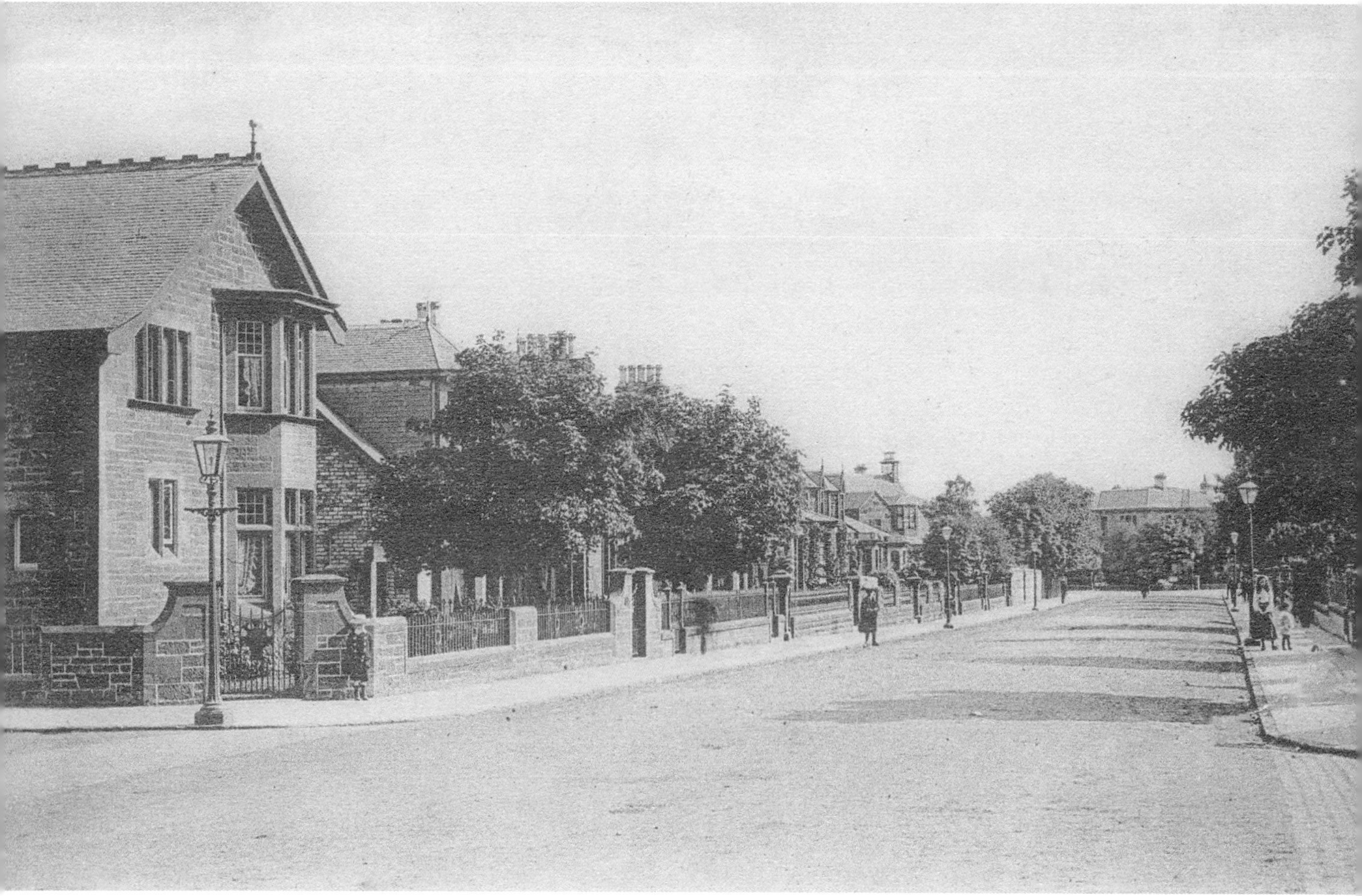

South Hamilton Street

South Hamilton Street was laid out in a straight line, linking Portland Road with Dundonald Road. On the north side of Portland Road it continues as North Hamilton Street. Both streets are lined with bungalows, many in blonde sandstone at the northern end, those to the south in red sandstone, and semi-detached homes, as well as some terraced homes in North Hamilton Street. Originally named Great Hamilton Street, the road was later divided into North and South sections. The land on which the street was built was originally owned by the Hamiltons. Initially, South Hamilton Street only extended as far as the old Kilmarnock to Troon railway line, roughly around number 24, before being extended. In South Hamilton Street is the Portland Bowling Club, established on 10 July 1860. Originally it only had one green, but a second was added. Predating the green are the cottages known as Springgrove (occupied by John Fleming in the 1860s), Ivy (Alexander Boyd in the 1860s), Hope and Summerlea (at one time the home of Rev Robert Gibson). Number 42, seen on the left of the picture, is located at the corner of South Hamilton Place and was for a time Kilmarnock Nursing Association Home. The building is a double-storey sandstone block, with a bay window to the main street and an arched doorway facing South Hamilton Place. Kilmarnock Nursing Association for the Sick Poor was formed in 1889 and the first nurse employed was a Miss Robin, a fully qualified Queen's Nurse. The association was affiliated to Queen Victoria's Jubilee Institute for Nursing. By 1898 a fourth nurse was taken on. At number 57 John P. Dickson lived until his death in 1939. He was editor of the *Kilmarnock Standard* for almost thirty years. Number 63, which is joined to a house in Dundonald Road, was the home of James Scott Hay (1871-1929), an Edinburgh-born architect, partner for a time with Gabriel Steel. He is known to have designed a few Kilmarnock buildings, including 90-94 Titchfield Street (1902), Auchenheath in Dundonald Road (1909) and Kirklandside Hospital, also erected in 1909. At the north end of the street, but with a Portland Road address, was the home of another architect, Thomas Smellie, the glazed upper floor being his studio.

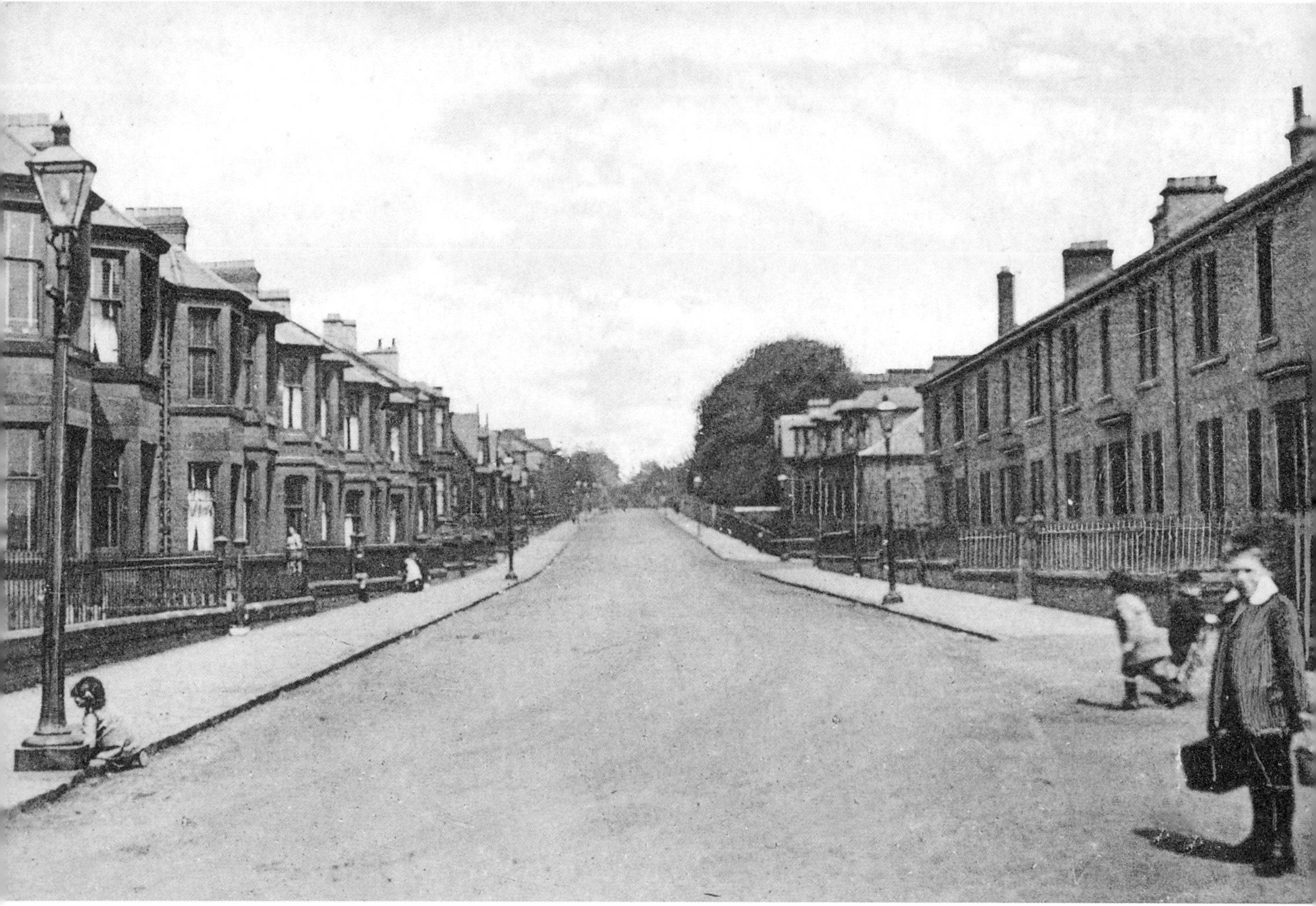

Glebe Road

Glebe Road was built to link Robertson Place and Welbeck Street to the south, with London Road to the north. The west side of the street, at the southern end, was built first of all, along with Arbuckle Street, which joins it from the left. The houses on the left with the bay windows were erected before 1896. Arbuckle Street follows, and then the buildings beyond, with the dormer windows facing the street. Most of the buildings were erected of red sandstone. The terrace on the right was built sometime after 1896. The street gets its name from being built on the lands originally belonging to the minister, and the Laigh Kirk Manse existed here before the street was laid out. The manse was sold in 1929 and latterly became an Occupational Centre before it was demolished and a new centre built on the site. This, in turn, has been demolished and in its place Glebe Court, consisting of ten houses, was built on the site by Klin Homes. Prior to the Glebe being developed, it was often used as the site for the annual cattle show of Kilmarnock Farmers' Society (established in 1793). At number 1, which is located at the corner with London Road, the distinguished neurologist and specialist in nervous diseases, Sir James Purves-Stewart (1869-1949), lived from 1942 for a few years. He was later to live in the lighthouse at Beachy Head. He was noted for his book, *Diagnosis of Nervous Diseases*, which went through numerous editions. Many of the other houses in the road were occupied by businessmen and professionals in the town, such as headmaster Thomas Amos (at number 19); James Brown of Hugh Lauder & Co. (17); James B. Tannahill (d. 1938), director of Kilmarnock Football Club (25); and David Murray, Rector of Kilmarnock Academy (7). At the southern end of the road, near the junction with Robertson Place, stood a four-storey building used by Irvinebank Dyeworks Ltd as a finishing and despatch building. Their main factory was located on the south side of New Mill Road. The Glebe Road building caught fire on 28 April 1942 and the building partially collapsed. Sparks set the Spiritualist Church in Gilmour Street alight, and it was destroyed too.

DEPTH OF WATER IN FEET.
GLENFIELD & KENNEDY LIMITED
MAKERS
KILMARNOCK
0 1 2 3 4 5 6 7 8 9 10 11 12 13 14 15 16

Glenfield & Kennedy

The photograph shows a collection of electrically-operated sluice valves within a building at Glenfield & Kennedy's factory. The firm was founded in 1899 when the businesses of Glenfield Company and Kennedy's Patent Water Meter Company were merged. The former business was established in 1865 as the Glenfield Iron Company, manufacturing iron castings for the water meter company (founded in 1863). Both firms had been established by Thomas Kennedy (1797-1874) who had moved to Kilmarnock from Argyll, initially running a watchmakers and gunsmiths. He patented his water meter in 1852, solving a long-standing problem. His nephew, also Thomas Kennedy (1838-1917) also served as a company director. The factory was located in the south-east quadrant of Glencairn Square, the Glenfield name coming from an old printworks on the site. In the early 1900s, a large extension was erected on the east side of the Kilmarnock Water, accessed from the original works by footbridges across the river. In 1921 Centrifugal Castings Ltd. was established as a subsidiary. Another subsidiary, British Pitometer Company was formed in 1923. In 1938 the firms won a £1 million contract to design, make and install flood gates for the London underground. In 1940 the company manufactured the wave-making machine that was installed in Kilmarnock Baths. On 3 June 1942 King George VI and Queen Elizabeth visited the Glenfield & Kennedy works. By 1951 the company had grown to employ 2,500 workers, but from then on went into decline. The company lost its local control in 1966 when it was taken over by the Crane organisation. The business was placed in receivership in 1977 but in November it was taken over by the Neptune International Corporation of Atlanta. The workforce had by this time shrunk to around 400. The company was sold to its local management in 1981 and the Glenfield and Kennedy name was reinstated. A considerable part of the older premises, including the offices in Low Glencairn Street, were demolished in 1982, the site being developed for small industrial units. This left the newer premises off Queen's Drive. In 1985 the company was taken over by Biwater and operated under the Biwater Valves name. In 1996 Biwater sold the company, which was later renamed Glenfield Valves Ltd, since 2001 owned by the AVK Group.

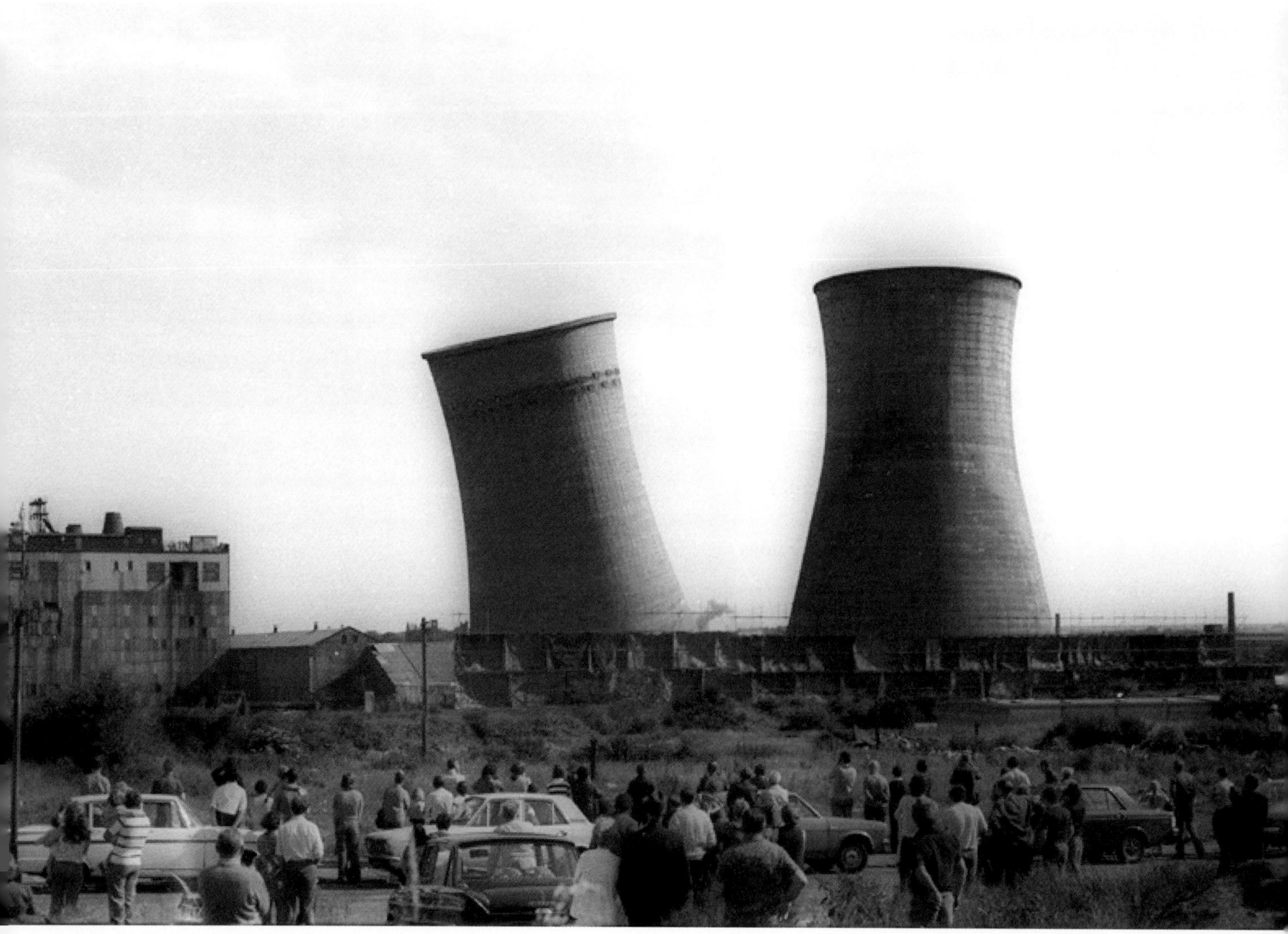

Kilmarnock Power Station

Kilmarnock electricity generating station was located at the bottom end of Low Glencairn Street, on a site previously occupied by Irvinebank Engine Works. A short Greenholm Street led into the works, which also incorporated the tramway depot. In fact, it was the council's keenness to have a tramway system that led to the creation of the power station. An act of parliament was obtained in 1903 to allow the erection of the station and formation of a tramway from Beansburn to Riccarton, with a branch to Hurlford. The first tram ran on 10 December 1903, driven by the 8th Lord Howard de Walden. The trams only lasted until 15 December 1926, losing the burgh money, but the power station was successful, and supplied electricity for street lighting and domestic use for many years. From 1904 until 1913 the supply was direct current, at 480 volts. In March 1914 a mixed pressure turbine was installed, allowing three phase electricity to be generated. In the same year the company supplied electricity to Troon, Irvine, Galston, Newmilns and Darvel for the first time. In 1917 the generating machinery was replaced by new turbines. In 1923 the power station became part of the Ayrshire Electricity Board. In 1927 an agreement was entered into between burghs of Kilmarnock and Greenock to give a bulk supply of electricity to Paisley, and transmission lines were erected between the three places. A new administrative building was erected in 1929. The generating station was connected to the National Grid in 1932. In 1938-39 a large cooling tower was erected on the opposite side of the River Irvine from the main works, on the site of what had been Riccarton & Craigie Railway Station. The first sod was cut by a silver spade on 7 April 1938. The second tower of what was locally called the 'milk bottles', was erected in 1942. In May 1952 an explosion at the works resulted in the death of three men in the switch room, plus a further two in hospital. During the Second World War the SAS used the power station to practise placing charges on generators. The power station continued to supply electricity to the grid until the 1970s. The towers remained for some time, before being demolished in June 1976.

A Look Back at KILMARNOCK ~ page 73

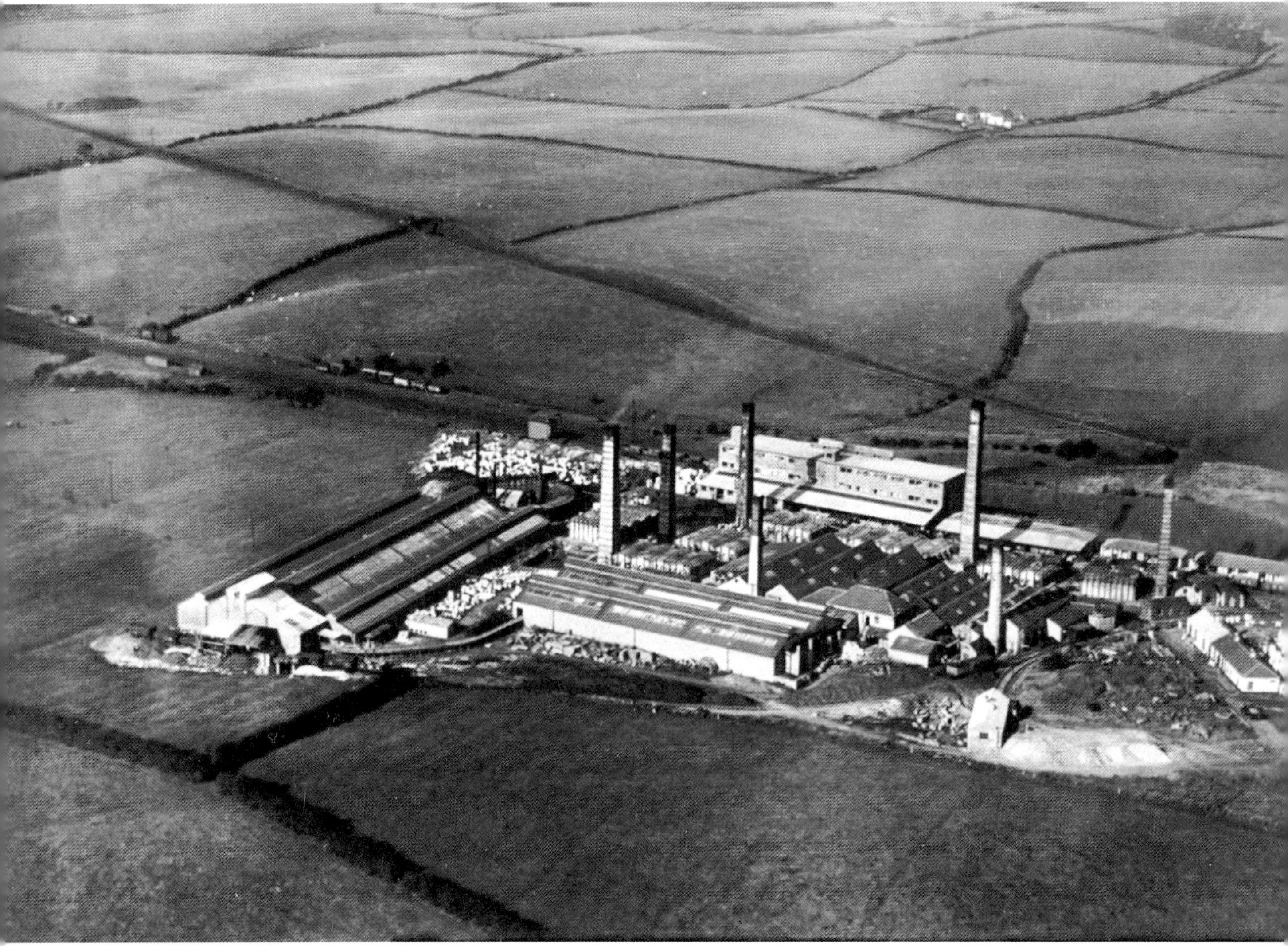

Bonnyton Fireclay Works

The Bonnyton Fireclay Works were established on the west side of Kilmarnock, on the south side of the Dalry and Kilmarnock railway line, to the west of the Western Road, though the works preceded this. It is thought the business was established around 1876 by John Gilmour & Co. on the site of Southhook Colliery No. 1 Pit. The business went bankrupt in 1883 and it appears to have been taken over by Anderson, Gilmour & Co. Sidings from the main line led into the works, allowing delivery of coal and clay and the export of finished products. In 1899 Gilmour, Morton & Co. Ltd. took over. In October of the same year, the works suffered a serious fire, when three drying sheds were burned down as a result of overheating stoves. The business went into liquidation again in 1908, at which time there were 400,000 enamelled bricks in stock. The works were taken over by Southhook and Shawsrigg Fire Clay Co. Ltd. and by 1935 by Southhook Potteries Ltd. The first rotary gas-fired kiln to be installed in Ayrshire was erected at Bonnyton Works in 1925, and after an experimental period it proved so successful that a second kiln was installed in 1930. The company manufactured white glazed sanitary ware, and amongst their popular items were the 'Espevit' closet set, comprising of a toilet pan and water tank. Wall-mounted sinks and basins were also manufactured, in addition to larger urinals that were commonly installed in gentlemen's toilets. As well as sanitary ware, the company also manufactured glazed brick and wall tiles, 'all in the finest enamelled fireclay'. A fairly unique example of a building incorporating Southhook glazed bricks can be found at 21-29 North Hamilton Street, where a terrace of houses erected in 1883 has a frontage of white bricks. These houses were designed by Robert Ingram and are known locally as the 'Cheeny Buildings'. It wasn't only white-glazed items that were produced – the company also made firebricks, sewage and drain pipes and other unglazed goods. At one time around 500 workers were employed here. By the early 1970s the company was known as Howie-Southhook Ltd. The factory was closed around that time and the buildings cleared by 1973. The site is currently occupied by Southhook Industrial Estate and the houses of Margaret Parker Avenue.

A Look Back at KILMARNOCK ~ *page 75*

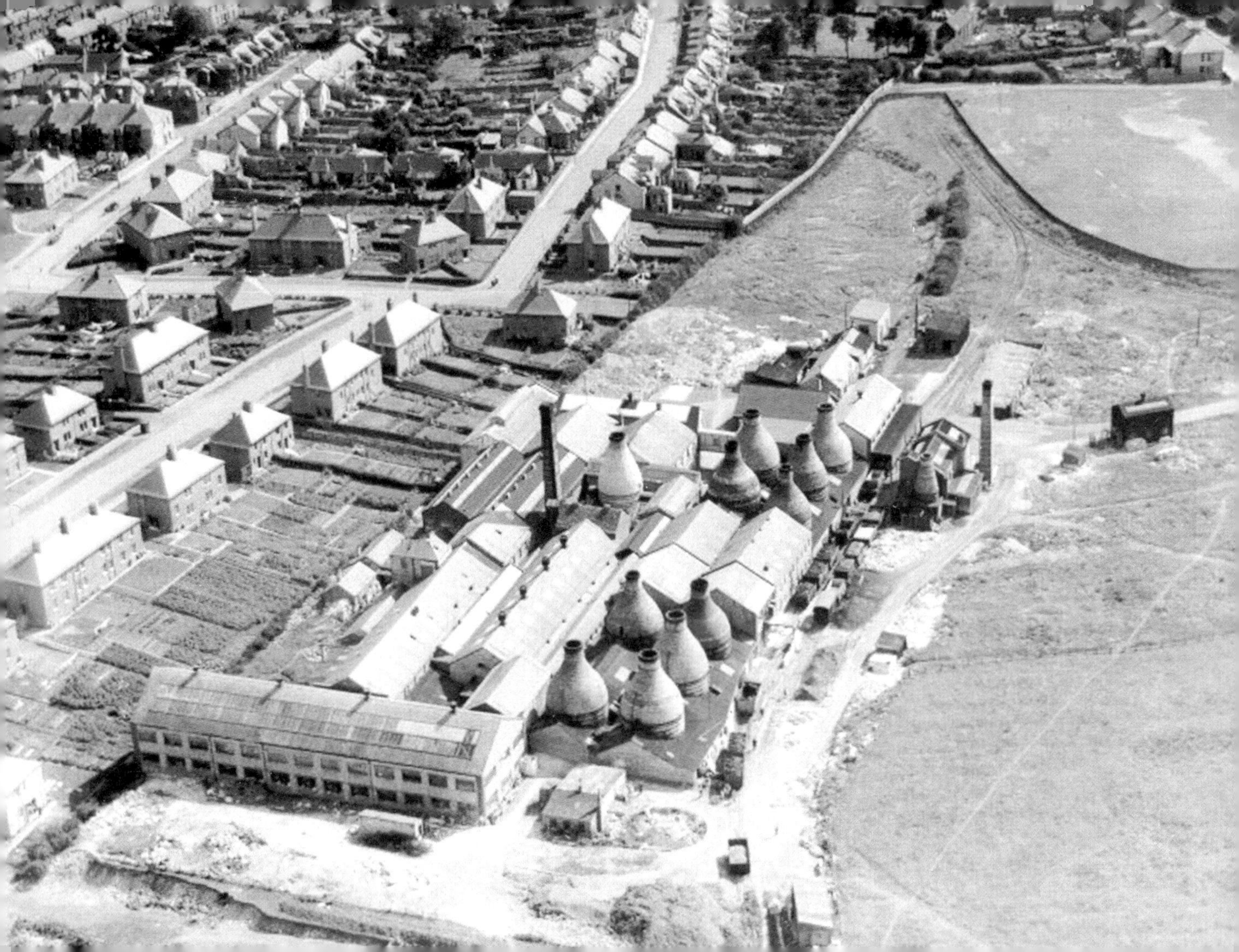

Longpark Sanitary Pottery

Viewed from the air, looking south, this was the Longpark Pottery. It was named after the elongated field in which it was built. The works were established in the 1880s on land adjoining the Hillhead Fireclay Works, previously Hillhead Brickworks. The works were taken over by James and Matthew Craig, sons of Matthew Craig, who ran the Dean Quarry. Hillhead fireclay works were closed in the early twentieth century and the various buildings demolished, leaving the open ground seen to the right of the right-hand chimney in the picture. J. & M. Craig became a limited company in 1896. The business also owned the Hillhead Colliery, Perceton Fire Clay Works (Irvine), Perceton Collieries, as well as the Lilliehill Fire Clay Works at Dunfermline. In 1906 the firm was reorganised as J. & M. Craig (Kilmarnock) Ltd, but it was liquidated in 1916. The company was taken over by Messrs Shanks of Barrhead in 1918. At one time there were around 300 employees at the factory. The pottery produced toilet bowls, wash-basins, bathroom fittings and other sanitary wares. An old advertisement of 1885 lists more of the products: 'The Shields' flush-out closet, white-enamelled sinks, Buchan's patent ventilating drain traps, sewer traps, etc. The Hillhead works made coloured earthenware, such as farm troughs and chimney cans. In 1950 the welfare committee built their own community centre, the hall of which measured 80 feet by 30 feet. In September 1981, the owners, Armitage Shanks (which the firm had become in 1969), closed the pottery, with the loss of 180 jobs. It was Scotland's last sanitary pottery. To the left of the pottery can be seen the council housing estate of Craig Avenue and Longpark Avenue, both named after the works. Hill Street is to the top-right of the image, with the Hill Street recreation ground, now occupied by the flats of Rosebank Place. The site of the pottery has been built over by housing, with the works occupied by Bath Street and Hillpark Drive. Even Craig Avenue was rebuilt with newer houses, named Graithnock Drive. This was in honour of the novelist, William McIlvanney, who set some of his works in the fictional town of Graithnock, said to be based on Kilmarnock.

Kilmarnock Infirmary

The old hospital that served Kilmarnock and district was located on the hillside above the bottom of Wellington Street. The original block, seen to the right, was designed by William Railton. The foundation stone was laid in September 1867 and on 24 September the following year the hospital was ready to take in its first patients. Built at a cost of £4,146, it originally had 24 beds. Adjoining the hospital was Mount Pleasant House, in whose grounds the infirmary had been built, used for administration services, but this was demolished and new wings were added, more than tripling in size the facility. A new ward for children was added in 1891, at a cost of £4,100, most of which was funded by Dowager Lady Howard de Walden, and additions were made in 1893 and a Fevers Block in 1899. On Saturday 19 May 1923 the hospital was extended once more, when the new wards, dining rooms, kitchen, mortuary and administration block were opened by Miss Finnie. Plans for this had started before the war. The additions were designed by Sir John Burnett, but he failed to attend due to a motor breakdown. He consulted Dr Mackintosh of the Western Infirmary, Glasgow, before producing his plans. This brought the number of beds up to 130. In 1922 the infirmary spent an average of £8 17s per patient. In the 1930s a new recreation hall and lecture theatre were added. The hospital, which was very cramped on its town-centre site, was for many years identified as suitable for a replacement. Plans to merge Ayr County Hospital and the infirmary in a new building at Grassyards Road were mooted, but came to nought due to the outbreak of the Second World War. The creation of the National Health Service in 1948 resulted in the infirmary coming under national control. The infirmary was closed in September 1982 when Crosshouse Hospital was opened. The infirmary sat empty for a number of years, with plans for demolition refused, A nursing home proposal failed and in the summer of 1994 the building went on fire and was thereafter demolished.

Acknowledgments

I would like to thank a few people who have kindly supplied images that have been used in this book. They include Bill Howie, Moira Rothnie and Marco Sinforiani. The other photographs are part of the author's own collection of images. I would also like to thank the many people who have supplied information to me over the years, or else pointed me in the right direction for this, the resultant notes and references being filed away just in case they are used in a book at
some time in the future.